THE NONPROFIT
LEGAL
LANDSCAPE

Edited by Thomas K. Hyatt

BOARDSOURCE
Building Effective Nonprofit Boards

Formerly the National Center for Nonprofit Boards

OBER|KALER
A Professional Corporation
Attorneys at Law

Library of Congress Cataloging-in-Publication Data

The nonprofit legal landscape / by Ober Kaler.
        p. cm.
        ISBN 1-58686-044-5 (pbk.)

1. Nonprofit organizations--Law and legislation--United States. I. Ober, Kaler, Grimes & Shriver. II. BoardSource (Organization) III. Title.

        KF1388.N67 2005
        346.73'064--dc22
        2004026759

© 2005 BoardSource.
First printing, January 2005.
ISBN 1-58686-044-5

Published by BoardSource
1828 L Street, NW, Suite 900
Washington, DC 20036

Additionally, BoardSource would like to thank Dennis Bass for his hard work and commitment in the developmental editing of this text.

BoardSource, formerly the National Center for Nonprofit Boards, is the premier resource for practical information, tools and best practices, training, and leadership development for board members of nonprofit organizations worldwide. Through our highly acclaimed programs and services, BoardSource enables organizations to fulfill their missions by helping build strong and effective nonprofit boards.

BoardSource provides assistance and resources to nonprofit leaders through workshops, training, and our extensive Web site, www.boardsource.org. A team of BoardSource governance consultants works directly with nonprofit leaders to design specialized solutions to meet organizations' needs and assists nongovernmental organizations around the world through partnerships and capacity building. As the world's largest, most comprehensive publisher of materials on nonprofit governance, BoardSource offers a wide selection of books, videotapes, and CDs. BoardSource also hosts the BoardSource Leadership Forum, bringing together approximately 800 governance experts, board members, and chief executives of nonprofit organizations from around the world.

Created out of the nonprofit sector's critical need for governance guidance and expertise, BoardSource is a 501(c)(3) nonprofit organization that has provided practical solutions to nonprofit organizations of all sizes in diverse communities. In 2001, BoardSource changed its name from the National Center for Nonprofit Boards to better reflect its mission. Today, BoardSource has more than 15,000 members and has served more than 75,000 nonprofit leaders.

For more information, please visit our Web site, www.boardsource.org, e-mail us at mail@boardsource.org, or call us at 800-883-6262.

Have You Used These BoardSource Resources?

For an up-to-date list of publications and information about current prices, membership, and other services, please call BoardSource at 800-883-6262 or visit our Web site at www.boardsource.org.

Contents

Foreword

This guidebook is the result of a collaborative effort by the attorneys who comprise the Nonprofits Practice Group at Ober|Kaler, as well as Firm attorneys in related fields of law. The book reflects the desire of our attorneys to make the core principles of the law that apply to nonprofit organizations more accessible and easier to understand, and to make their interplay more apparent. The subject areas discussed herein — both in number and in breadth — reveal the increasing sophistication and complexity involved in the operation of a nonprofit organization.

We thank the individual authors for their time and commitment in preparing this guidebook. Each is an outstanding practitioner, a good colleague, and a supporter of the important missions to which nonprofit organizations are dedicated. Thanks also go to Ober|Kaler's management committee and the firm's chair, John Wolf, for their support of this important project. We offer appreciation and gratitude to the BoardSource blue-ribbon publication team: Claire Perella, George Gates, Dennis Bass, and Marla Bobowick, for their insight, direction, and endless patience.

Finally, we extend our gratitude to our nonprofit clients and friends. We have learned from you, we have been inspired by you, and we dedicate this guidebook to you. We look forward to our continued mutual endeavors in promoting education and improving operation and governance in the nonprofit sector.

Thomas K. Hyatt
December, 2004

Introduction

WHY SHOULD DIRECTORS AND MANAGERS BE CONCERNED ABOUT THE LEGAL LANDSCAPE?

At first glance, it might seem that a book of this length and complexity, about a potpourri of legal topics, would be of little use to a director or executive of a nonprofit organization. Why not rely on the expertise of line staff or hire outside professionals or counsel to advise the top policy-makers of the organization?

Because, as President Harry Truman said, "The buck stops here." You and your fellow directors and executives are the persons who are ultimately responsible for the actions — good and bad — of your nonprofit. If you are the responsible persons, then you need to be in control. It is impossible to have that control without a passing familiarity with the important legal issues for nonprofits so that — at the very least — you know what questions to ask staff or outside counsel and what options are available in different situations.

The Nonprofit Legal Landscape can serve directors and executives as a useful reference tool for the most important laws and legal concepts that require their awareness. When confronted with a legal issue involving your nonprofit, you can refer quickly to *The Nonprofit Legal Landscape* in order to bring yourself rapidly to the next level of understanding.

Increasingly, nonprofit organizations are operating in a legal and quasi-legal environment. To an unprecedented degree, nonprofit groups are being subjected to intensifying regulation by all levels of government: federal, state, and local. Regulators, who used to focus primarily on for-profit companies' operations, are now using their public authority to examine, investigate, and change nonprofits as well. Legal concepts that used to apply solely to profit-making businesses are being expanded by courts and state attorneys general to cover nonprofit groups. Federal and state laws regulate in detail how nonprofits can be created, governed, and operated — and many impose significant penalties for noncompliance, including the possible loss of tax-exempt status. While much of this expanded scrutiny of nonprofits is healthy and welcome, it poses new challenges to nonprofit board members and chief executives.

This text will lead readers through this legal maze in two important ways: 1) by helping to avoid legal problems before they begin, and 2) by teaching how to cope with such problems once they have arisen. For example, you are in a board meeting and you learn that your nonprofit has paid a substantial sum to develop a new logo. Because you have read Chapter 5 of *The Nonprofit Legal Landscape* on intellectual property, you know to ask whether trademark protection of the new logo has been sought in order to avoid possible infringement of others' marks, as well as to secure and preserve through trademark protection a new, valuable asset of your nonprofit. Your basic knowledge — and a few well-phrased questions — may very well save the organization from problems and losses down the road.

Likewise, *The Nonprofit Legal Landscape* can help you cope with problems after they have appeared. At another board meeting, you might hear that the organization's contribution to the retirement plan of several senior executives was dramatically increased last year. Since you've read Chapter 7 on employee benefits law, you know that such "discrimination" in favor of executives and against lower-paid employees may be illegal in the type of retirement plan your nonprofit has established. Your words of warning may alert the organization to seek legal counsel before the imbalance in the plan evolves into a legal and tax nightmare.

The personal liability to which you subject yourself as a member of a nonprofit board of directors is another reason to utilize this book. As described in Chapter 3, directors have specific and well-defined duties to the nonprofit they serve, violation of which can subject them to liability. And, while there are many caveats and protections available to board members, it is still possible to be held personally liable for some actions of the board as a whole or of the nonprofit's staff.

The Nonprofit Legal Landscape is organized as a soup-to-nuts guide beginning with the options and advantages available for organizing a nonprofit, as well as the all-important tax considerations that are fundamental to any nonprofit. In Chapter 3, directors' legal duties and responsibilities are thoroughly examined, and liability and indemnification explained. The next chapter explains the significant lobbying and electioneering restrictions that tax-exempt nonprofits must observe — and which are easy for directors and executives to run afoul of. Protection and preservation of a nonprofit's valuable intellectual property follow.

Substantial space is devoted in this book to various facets of employment and employee benefits law. Nonprofits are bound by a burgeoning number of statutes and cases that affect the employer-employee relationship. Staying out of employment-related troubles can be a major preoccupation of nonprofits; these chapters tell you how to do that. The increasing importance of immigration law to nonprofits — both those that wish to hire noncitizens and those that wish to serve noncitizen clients — is also explored. Larger nonprofits will also want to take heed of the restrictions on operation identified in the chapter on antitrust law.

Finally, the last chapters look at various ways a nonprofit can cope with an investigation or lawsuit by government, client, or employee, and describes the process for each.

The Nonprofit Legal Landscape is designed to give you a yardstick against which you can measure the practices and policies of your nonprofit and to highlight areas that may need your further examination or attention. We hope it achieves these goals so that, as a responsible director or executive of a nonprofit, you can be fully aware of the legal environment within which your organization operates — for its sake, as well as your own.

1.
Organizing a Nonprofit

Patrick K. O'Hare

Charitable and other nonprofit activities can be undertaken by like-minded individuals without any legal form or organization — and, in fact, this is how many nonprofit organizations get started. But in the long run, most groups will not find this method satisfactory because it does not protect the individual participants from liability; it is clumsy to administer; and it may preclude tax exemption and the associated benefit of tax-deductible contributions. To avoid these problems, most nonprofits choose to organize themselves as a corporation — a legal form of organization that is available to nonprofits under every state's laws.

A corporation is actually an artificial creation of state law, but it offers some very desirable advantages, such as liability protection for its members, directors, and officers (they are not liable for the acts of the corporation), ease and predictability of governance, and the ability to both qualify for tax exemption and to attract tax-deductible donations or membership dues. (State laws permit other types of organization, but most of them — unincorporated associations, limited liability companies, and different variations of partnerships — have significant drawbacks as vehicles for nonprofit activities.)

State statutes and common law govern the formation, organization, and ongoing operations of corporations. This chapter will summarize the key corporate law principles applicable to nonprofit corporations, and focus on the role and responsibilities that board members have in overseeing a nonprofit corporation's activities.

First Steps in Forming a Nonprofit Corporation

Preparing the Articles of Incorporation

Nonprofit corporations are created by one or more persons (called *incorporators*) who prepare and file the corporation's "articles of incorporation" with the appropriate state agency. Each state's law prescribes both the content and form of this document. The articles of incorporation are prepared to satisfy two audiences — the state and, assuming some category of tax exemption will be applied for, the United States Internal Revenue Service (IRS). Accordingly, the most important part of the articles — the entity's purposes — must fall within the statutory list of purposes for which nonprofits in that state may be organized. (Purposes may be broad or narrow, but should be carefully composed so as not to constrain future operations or activities of the nonprofit.) The articles must also contain the key requirements to make the entity eligible for tax exemption.

State law typically requires that nonprofit corporations be organized for some type of charitable or other benevolent purpose that benefits society at large, and that the corporation's activities and assets be dedicated to achieving those designated purposes. This is the key difference between corporations organized for profit and those organized as nonprofits: The former exist to make profits that are distributed to members, stockholders, or owners; the latter must devote all revenues and profits to charitable purposes. (Although nonprofits are allowed to generate *profits* — more precisely, an excess of revenues over expenses — the profits cannot be distributed to members or individuals.)

Once the articles are filed with the appropriate state agency, the state will return either a certificate, charter, or other document (analogous to a birth certificate) recognizing the nonprofit's legal existence and the effective date of its incorporation. At this point, the role of the incorporators is completed.

CREATING BYLAWS

The articles of incorporation will identify the initial directors, or board members, of the corporation. These individuals must organize the corporation by adopting its bylaws, appointing the initial officers, and completing the other routine tasks (e.g., securing a federal employee identification number) that will enable the corporation to commence its activities.

The bylaws of a corporation, much like a state's constitution, outline its governance and general authority levels within the organization. Because bylaws take time and effort to change, detailed operational issues and procedures should not be included; only the basic structure of the way in which the directors want the nonprofit to function should be outlined in the document. (Please see Suggested Resources on page 135 for more information on how to draft bylaws.)

The most important question to be answered in the bylaws is whether the nonprofit corporation will or will not have members. When a corporation has members, those members usually have the right to elect the board members of the corporation and to vote on other important matters, such as amendments to the articles of incorporation or bylaws and fundamental corporate changes (e.g., mergers and dissolutions). The definition and specific rights of members should be spelled out in the bylaws. If the corporation has no members, the board members are a self-perpetuating group that elects its own successors.

The bylaws also set forth the provisions for election and removal of directors and officers; directors' qualifications for office; the length of directors' and officers' terms; and, if desired, a staggering of the directors' terms to prevent all terms from expiring at the same time.

Ex officio directors — individuals who serve in a position "by virtue of this office" — add a layer of complexity. It is not uncommon, for example, for the most senior-level employee such as the executive director to serve ex officio. While *Roberts Rules of Order* and other governance resources state that ex officio directors usually have the right to vote unless specified otherwise, there is often confusion on this point. Therefore, the bylaws should specify clearly whether such ex officio directors may vote or not, and whether the presence of a nonvoting, ex officio director counts towards a quorum. To avoid confusion and contention, most nonprofits limit the number of ex officio members on their boards, and those who do serve as ex officio do not usually count toward a quorum.

The bylaws will typically contain the particulars regarding notice and meetings of the board and members (if any), describe the officers' positions and their duties, detail the committee structure, and specify the method of amending the bylaws. Bylaws are not static and should be reviewed and amended if they create procedural problems, fall short of governance best practices, or if they are inconsistent with actual operations. While bylaws should not be altered frequently — and the time-consuming provisions for changing them should deter that tendency — it is a good practice to review bylaws periodically and adjust them in response to the organization's growth and change and to clarify any confusion that may exist.

OFFICERS: WHO SHOULD BE ELECTED, AND HOW?

Officers exist by virtue of the relevant state's statute, which typically requires that a corporation have at least two officers: a president and a secretary. Additional officers, e.g., one or more vice presidents, a treasurer, and assistant officers, may also be authorized by statute. Generally, two or more officer positions can be held by the same person, except those of president and secretary. Many corporations elect to have a "chair" of the board in addition to the president. This is permitted, and the bylaws should make it clear what the duties of each are. If there is no "chair," the bylaws should provide that the president will chair all meetings of the board. If there is no "president," the description of the duties of the "chair" should include those of president, to satisfy the state requirement that the corporation have a president.

All duties of the officers are prescribed in the bylaws. Corporate officers' identities are required to be disclosed in state annual filings, and many third parties will insist that various transaction documents be executed only by one or more specified officers (even though a legally valid delegation of authority could be made to an employee). Officers of a corporation should not be confused with senior management employees. Senior management personnel usually hold jobs titled "chief executive officer," "executive director," "chief financial officer," and so on. Unless the board of directors specifically appoints the employee to an officer or assistant officer position, such person is considered an employee and not an officer of the board. This distinction matters for several reasons. Bylaws usually require that only board members are qualified to serve as officers, precluding the appointment of an executive director as "president," unless the individual is also elected a board member. Additionally, officers generally owe a higher fiduciary duty to the corporation than do employees. Knowing which is which is important for purposes of liability insurance (which might only cover officers and directors, or board members) and indemnity obligations (which might extend to employees as well, but without the insurance funds to support the obligation).

DELEGATING TO COMMITTEES AND MANAGERS

Directors are permitted to delegate their responsibilities under certain circumstances. Despite any delegation, however, the board still retains responsibility for the overall operations and cannot avoid legal responsibility by claiming that mistakes were the fault of a committee, the executive director, or an officer. The board must satisfy itself through monitoring, oversight, and final approval of any recommendations that those to whom it delegates are using reasonable care and skill in exercising authority in the board's name.

One useful example of permissible delegation is the creation of board committees. Committees are of two types:

1. Those that are composed exclusively of directors who are delegated certain specified powers of the board of directors (subject to limitations in any state statute); common examples are an audit committee and an investment committee, both of which tackle subjects that may be overly complex for the entire board, or an executive committee that may be empowered to act between board meetings; and

2. Those composed of both directors and nondirectors who only advise the board on governance issues and decision making.

Delegation also occurs when authority is given to appointed officers so they can take certain actions without prior approval of the full board. Delegation can likewise be made to management personnel, such as the executive director, who are not officers of the corporation. These delegations can be made in the bylaws, a board resolution, a written policy, or even in an employment agreement.

While the board is ultimately responsible for the operations of an organization, this does not mean that the board should be involved on a day-to-day basis in making operational decisions for the organization under normal circumstances. (Too much oversight can be just as bad as too little.) Instead, the board should 1) define the general direction for the organization and set applicable policies, 2) make major fiscal decisions, and 3) oversee organizational activities and ensure the overall health and ethical standing of the nonprofit. Other administrative decisions and daily operations should be left to competent staff.

MAINTAINING A CORPORATION IN GOOD STANDING

To ensure that a nonprofit's corporate existence is maintained, it is vital that important corporate formalities be observed. These formalities include holding member and board meetings when required; maintaining accurate corporate minutes; keeping the corporation's assets separate from those of other entities, including subsidiaries; and ensuring that any subsidiary board is actually involved in the operation of the subsidiary corporation and that the accounts of the subsidiary are properly maintained. In addition, required annual state filings should be made; in some states, failure to make such filings can result in dissolution of the corporation.

Unless the important formalities are observed, financial responsibility for acts taken by the corporation may fall on other entities and individuals. For example, continuing the operations of the corporation after dissolution caused by failing to make required annual filings can, in some states, deem the directors and officers personally liable for the acts of the corporation.

ENTERING INTO CONTRACTS

One of the most significant powers of any nonprofit corporation is its ability to enter into contracts with third parties. Usually, for the contract to be enforceable, the execution of a contract must be authorized by action of the board or by a properly authorized officer, employee, or agent who has been delegated the power to execute the agreement. Contracts may generally be oral or written; specifically, contracts dealing with real property, those which cannot be performed in one year, or those dealing with the sale of certain goods must be in writing. (And, as a general rule, contracts *should* be written in order to avoid the misunderstandings that can arise from oral agreements.) It is good nonprofit management to centralize all contracting authority and to specify a required level of officer, committee, or board approval — depending on the dollar amount of the contract. For example, a board might establish a $25,000 limit for approval of contracts by the executive director, with contracts between $25,000 and $50,000 requiring approval of the board's executive committee, and commitments above that amount coming to the full board for approval.

Because the corporation, not the board, is legally the contracting party, the corporation can be bound by the terms of a multiyear contract regardless of the desires of a future board. In other words, even though turnover in board membership may cause the board to question prior contracts, the new board will have to fulfill the contractual obligations created by previous boards.

Occasionally, an employee or officer may enter into a contract on behalf of the corporation without the required authority to do so. In this event, the corporation can ratify the action afterwards, should it wish to take advantage of the contract. Even if the corporation did not wish to do so, that contract might nonetheless be enforced against the corporation, to the extent that the other contracting party justifiably relied on the *apparent* authority of the employee or officer to execute the contract. Accordingly, it is critical for a nonprofit to exercise adequate control over its contracting activities so that it is not inadvertently made responsible for contractual obligations that it did not intend.

RECENT LEGAL DEVELOPMENTS AFFECTING NONPROFITS

The landmark corporate reform and accountability legislation of 2002, commonly referred to as "Sarbanes-Oxley," was aimed at curbing abuses of for-profit corporations. But two of the law's criminal provisions — prohibiting retaliation against whistleblowers and the destruction of documents — apply to nonprofit corporations.

Although Sarbanes-Oxley was not directed at nonprofits, the reforms in that legislation do have resonance for nonprofit organizations. And, in fact, Congress, state legislators, and state attorneys general are all actively considering applying the most important governance reforms of Sarbanes-Oxley to nonprofits. Thus, a brief review of its four most salient provisions is relevant:

1. For-profit corporate governing boards are now required to establish audit committees that are responsible for retaining and supervising the corporation's outside audit firm. The audit committee must be independent; that is, the chief executive, chief financial officer, and any board member who does business with the corporation is ineligible to sit on the committee. The corporation must also disclose whether the members of the audit committee are financial experts and, if not, why not — making it vital to have directors with independent financial expertise.

2. Both the chief executive and chief financial officer must certify that the corporation's annual financial report is accurate and that there are systems of internal controls in place to ensure that material matters are brought to their attention. They must also declare that they have disclosed to the auditors any deficiencies in internal controls, as well as any fraud involving management.

3. Compensation packages for senior executives may no longer include personal loans from the corporation. Personal loans are also prohibited to directors and officers. (They may already be prohibited under some states' laws.) Additionally, corporations must adopt a code of conduct for senior financial officers.

4. To address perceived conflicts of interest of auditing firms that also supply consulting services to clients, the independent auditor for a corporation may not provide consulting services to that group in certain fields, including bookkeeping, human resources, and investment services. An audit firm should also rotate the lead and reviewing audit partner for a corporation at least every five years.

While these requirements have yet to be applied to nonprofit corporations at the federal level, it is becoming increasingly difficult for nonprofits — especially those with significant resources, donations, and public visibility — to hold themselves to lesser standards than those that apply to their for-profit peers. Some nonprofits may choose voluntarily to adopt these provisions now in order to assure donors, charity watchdog groups, state regulators, and lenders of their adherence to the highest standards of fiscal accountability. (They may also do so to distinguish themselves favorably among competing organizations.)

ARE THERE OTHER FORMS OF NONPROFIT ORGANIZATIONS?

Although, as noted previously, joint ventures, limited liability companies, and partnerships are not as useful for initially organizing a nonprofit organization, they may at some point be useful for an organization to enhance and expand its activities in concert with other nonprofit or for-profit partners.

JOINT VENTURES

A joint venture is an undertaking by two or more persons or entities with the intent to carry out a single or one-time business enterprise for their mutual profit. Joint ventures can be organized as formal partnerships or limited liability companies. Even without such formal organization, joint ventures created by contract often have the legal status of a partnership, and the participants therein treated as partners.

Joint ventures have become more popular with tax-exempt nonprofit organizations because they can facilitate access to three important sectors: capital, markets, and expertise. For example, a nonprofit museum might seek the expertise of an experienced participant in a new venture, such as catalog sales. It could establish a joint venture with a for-profit catalog sales company to create and sell reproductions of items in the museum's collections — and to share the profits. Or a nonprofit organization might wish to construct its own headquarters building, but does not have sufficient capital (or may want to preserve its existing capital). The organization might seek out a for-profit development company and enter into a joint venture to construct a headquarters building and share the rental revenues from other tenants.

Similarly, a nonprofit may want to enter a new market where another entity is already well entrenched; in this case, the process of entering the market could be greatly eased by working in tandem with the other entity.

Below are brief descriptions of the forms that a joint venture may take, with the advantages of each:

- **A general partnership arrangement:** The only participants in a general partnership are general partners (those responsible for the management of the business) and each may contribute cash, property, or services in varying or equal amounts. General partners are typically equally liable for the debts and obligations of the partnership and all can be required to make additional capital contributions to the partnership when necessary. What makes a partnership arrangement attractive is the fact that it is a conduit entity, which is to say it does not pay taxes. Instead, the net revenue of the partnership passes through to the partners who are individually responsible for paying taxes on net income. Other tax advantages such as depreciation and interest deductions also pass through to the partners. These tax-related advantages, while not of much use to a nonprofit itself, may be very enticing to a potential for-profit partner.

- **A limited partnership:** This arrangement is one in which there are both general and limited partners. Essentially, limited partners are investors whose only function is to supply the partnership with capital. Their liability is limited to the amount of their capital contribution and they are generally not liable for additional capital unless the partnership agreement provides otherwise. Limited partners generally participate so as to achieve a return on their investment and to secure tax advantages. They cannot participate materially in the management of the entity.

- **A limited liability company (LLC):** This is a hybrid that combines the most attractive features of corporate and partnership organization. Thus, it is a conduit entity that does not pay taxes at the LLC level, but liability for all investors is limited to the amount of their capital contribution. All 50 states and the District of Columbia have enacted statutes permitting the creation of LLCs.

MERGERS AND AFFILIATIONS

Increased pressure to contain costs and to be as efficient as possible with donated funds is leading some nonprofits to consider merging or affiliating with others. Although somewhat uncommon, these combinations may take many forms, including a corporate merger or consolidation, an acquisition of assets, or an affiliation. There is no one right way to combine nonprofit organizations and the model chosen will depend on the needs and desires of the organizations involved, as well as the postcombination governance structure that is desired by the two entities.

In a merger or consolidation, the corporate existence of each of the merged entities disappears, and the surviving corporation becomes the owner of and responsible for all of the assets and liabilities (including contracts) of the entity being merged into it. The governing board of the successor entity may be comprised of the directors of both merging entities. In another scenario, the merged entity may retain its status as a semiautonomous division of the successor entity with its own advisory board of directors, although governance and control of the division would ultimately lie with the new entity's board of directors.

Another strategy is the sale of one nonprofit's assets to another nonprofit. An asset sale requires *consideration* for the assets that are purchased (which is often simply the assumption of some or all of the liabilities of the "selling" nonprofit). The asset sale, however, does not end the existence of the selling corporation. To do that, the board of directors of the selling nonprofit must formally terminate (i.e., dissolve and liquidate) the nonprofit corporation, following the requirements of the state's laws. (Please note that, in many states, the proposed sale of all of the assets of a nonprofit requires notice to the attorney general or other state regulators.)

MULTICORPORATE SYSTEMS

As the missions of nonprofits have become more complicated and compliance with the regulations to which they are subject becomes more difficult, some nonprofits have adopted a system of multiple, affiliated corporations — each with separate functions, activities, fundraising programs, and even tax statuses. Common examples include a nonprofit with a supporting foundation; a charitable nonprofit with a sister social welfare organization that is eligible to undertake lobbying activities; a nonprofit holding-company structure with a for-profit subsidiary; or a nonprofit with interests in one or more joint ventures.

It is beyond the scope of this text to elaborate on when these systems are appropriate and how each of them should be structured, other than to note that corporate and governance features must meet both corporate law and tax-exemption requirements, and they should utilize a structure that will be as efficient as possible. Implementing multicorporate structures takes significant time, needs strong constituent and management support, requires deft political handling in the creation of new director positions, and necessitates attention to numerous issues, including accounting concerns, state regulations, employee benefits, and human resources issues. Governance needs, such as consistent bylaws and committee structures, must also be addressed. Many entities elect to use outside facilitators to manage this process and engage legal counsel to assist in creating these structures.

There are many decisions to be made by the organizers of a nonprofit organization. Typically, a nonprofit organization is formed by a few leaders or an initial board of directors in consultation with legal counsel and accountants. The chief executive may have already been identified or may be hired later. As discussed in this chapter, this planning group will need to be familiar with the various decisions to be made regarding the state of incorporation, the form of business vehicle, and the type of tax-exempt status that will best serve the organization's needs. Once these initial important decisions have been made, the new nonprofit organization will rely upon counsel to create the organization, reserve its name, prepare initial bylaws, and file an application with the IRS for recognition of tax-exempt status. The organization's accountants will assist with obtaining an employer identification number, preparing an initial budget, and developing important financial data needed for the preparation of the organization's application for tax-exempt status. Thereafter, the initial board or leaders will need to go about the task of identifying the full complement of directors to serve on the first board. Thereafter, the full board of directors can tackle the important tasks of debating and adopting full bylaws that incorporate governance best practices. Throughout its life, the board will also address the ongoing organizational issues that come before it, such as whether and how to enter into joint ventures, and whether to merge or affiliate with other organizations.

QUESTIONS THE BOARD SHOULD ASK

- Do we have a process in place to review our legal documents from time to time?
- Should we consider conducting a legal audit of the organization?
- Have we incorporated due diligence into all of our processes?

2.
Tax Considerations for Nonprofits

Thomas K. Hyatt

Although an organization may have qualified for nonprofit status, it is important to recognize that nonprofit status is not synonymous with being tax exempt. Nonprofit status simply means that a group has met its state's requirements for that designation. It is entirely possible for a nonprofit organization to be taxed on its income. This is the case if the nonprofit has chosen not to apply for tax-exempt status (and therefore is not recognized as tax exempt) or if it is unable to qualify for tax-exempt status but continues to qualify as a nonprofit organization under state law. (The criteria that states require an entity to meet to qualify as a nonprofit are generally quite similar to those that are required under federal tax law to become tax exempt, but they are not always identical.)

Most nonprofits recognize the great benefit of federal tax-exempt status, and so, once organized as a nonprofit, they then pursue recognition of exemption. Nonprofit organizations will usually apply for exemption from state income tax as well. This is typically a less burdensome process and most states will automatically recognize exemption from state income tax if the nonprofit organization has already acquired recognition of its tax-exempt status from the IRS.

State income tax exemption, however, does not usually confer exemption from other state and local taxes, such as real property, personal property, and sales taxes. Separate applications must be made to state or local (county or city) governments for exemption from those levies. In recent years, state and local governments have become much more aggressive about trying to tax the real property of otherwise tax-exempt organizations. The standards for exemption for state or local property tax are typically much narrower than those for exemption from income taxation. Accordingly, a nonprofit organization may fully qualify as a charity under federal and state income tax law, but not under state or local property or sales tax laws. Nevertheless, it is worth considering application for exemption from those taxes because of the significant savings to be had for the nonprofit if exemption can be achieved.

Nearly all nonprofit organizations are able to qualify for exemption from federal income taxation. However, as a condition of receiving this exemption, nonprofit organizations become subject to substantial restrictions on their governance and operations in order to ensure that they are operating solely in furtherance of their stated nonprofit purposes. Federal tax law restricts how nonprofit organizations are governed, provides guidelines to be used in determining the compensation of key employees and agents, restricts the business opportunities available to them (and the manner in which they may be structured), and delineates their access to capital and contributions from donors. These restrictions will be further explored below.

There are several categories of tax exemption for nonprofit organizations available under the Internal Revenue Code (the "Code"). By far, the most common of these is status as a charitable organization described in Section 501(c)(3) of the Code. Two other common categories are social welfare organizations [Section 501(c)(4)] and trade associations [Section 501(c)(6)]. (Other, less commonly used categories of tax exemption include such varied possibilities as social clubs, labor organizations, employee benefit funds, political organizations, cemetery companies, credit unions, veterans' organizations, homeowners associations, and farmers' cooperatives.)

TAX EXEMPTION FOR CHARITABLE ORGANIZATIONS

A nonprofit may qualify for exemption from federal income tax as a *charitable* organization under Section 501(c)(3) if it is organized and operated exclusively for broadly defined charitable, religious, educational, scientific, or literary purposes. Tax-exempt status is recognized by the IRS upon the receipt of proof of qualification by the organization; this is accomplished by filing a completed Form 1023 with the IRS (forms and instructions are available online at www.irs.gov/eo). Note that, although other tax-exempt entities such as social welfare organizations and trade associations are not required to file an application for recognition of federal tax exemption, they nevertheless have the option to do so — and it is usually advisable to file a Form 1024 in order to receive written confirmation from the IRS of such organizations' tax status.

To qualify as a charitable organization, an organization's articles of incorporation must limit its purposes to one or more of those enumerated above, and must not expressly empower it to engage, other than as an insubstantial part of its activities, in activities that are not in furtherance of those purposes. (This requirement will not be met if the limitations are found only in the organization's bylaws.) In addition, the articles of incorporation must provide that, in the event of dissolution of the organization, its assets will be distributed for an exempt purpose or to federal, state, or local government for a public purpose. These requirements are collectively referred to as the *organizational test*.

In addition to meeting the organizational test, nonprofits must also meet an *operational test*. That is, the organization must be operated exclusively for one or more of the specified exempt purposes. However, the IRS interprets "exclusively" to mean "primarily." Therefore, a nonprofit will satisfy the operational test if it engages primarily in activities that accomplish its exempt purposes. It will fail the test, on the other hand, if a substantial part of its activities is not in furtherance of those purposes.

A second aspect of the operational test is both a prohibition against private benefit and a proscription against private inurement. These are the most fundamental operating restrictions that are placed on charitable organizations. Each will be discussed separately below.

The organization must be engaged in activities that further *public* purposes rather than *private* interests. Obviously, on occasion there may be some incidental benefit to a private interest by a nonprofit; for example, an exempt hospital indirectly serves the private interests of its physicians. But the IRS is concerned with the *primary* purpose of the organization: If serving private interests is only incidental to the nonprofit's accomplishment of its charitable purpose, then the organization will meet this test. In the case of a hospital, the benefits to its physicians are incidental to the hospital's work to achieve its primary public purpose of providing health care to the public.

Second, the organization's net earnings must not inure in whole or in part to the benefit of private shareholders or individuals. IRS regulations define a private shareholder or individual as any person having a personal and private interest in the activities of the organization. Read literally, the "no part" requirement means there is no *de minimus* exception to the private inurement proscription. If *any* private inurement is present, tax-exempt status will fail. (In contrast, the private benefit prohibition described above has been applied so as to permit incidental private benefit without penalty.)

The IRS has limited the application of the no-private-inurement rule, for the most part, to "insiders": individuals who have a personal and private interest in the activities of the exempt organization and have the authority to direct the organization to provide them a share of the net earnings. (It is often difficult to determine when the line is crossed that causes an individual to be considered an insider. The presence of control is the determining factor for the IRS, since it is the power to cause the organization to confer the improper benefit that is of concern.)

Federal tax law does not prohibit all dealings between a charitable organization and its insiders. Insiders may transact at arm's length with a charitable organization and receive reasonable compensation for goods or services provided to the organization without violating the rule against private inurement.

WHAT IS OUR PUBLIC CHARITY STATUS?

Qualification as a public charity is very advantageous for a nonprofit when applying for tax exemption. The advantages arise from the distinction made in the law between "public" and "private" charities. If a nonprofit cannot qualify as a public charity, it is classified under federal law as a private charity (called *private foundations*), though it is still tax exempt. But if a nonprofit can meet the criteria to be a public charity, it does not have to meet the many other requirements placed on private foundations, such as mandatory distribution of a part of its net investment assets each year, payment of an annual excise tax on its net investment income, adherence to substantial restrictions on the use of its funds (with severe penalties and taxes for violations), and burdensome reporting requirements.

To obtain the advantageous public charity status, a nonprofit must fall within certain categories of organizations that are responsive to and supported by the general public. The determination of public charity status for an organization will in some cases be automatic, as is the case for a hospital, church, or college; while for others, the nonprofit must qualify for public charity status by the nature and amount of its public support. The box on page 13 illustrates some examples.

WHAT IS A PUBLIC CHARITY?

There are six types of organizations that are automatically, by definition, public charities:

1. a church or a convention or association of churches;

2. an educational organization such as a school or college;

3. a hospital or medical research organization operated in conjunction with a hospital;

4. organizations operated for the benefit of certain state and municipal colleges and universities;

5. a governmental unit; and

6. a "publicly supported" organization.

A nonprofit can qualify in the latter category of publicly supported organizations if it normally receives a substantial portion of its support from a governmental unit or from the general public. Each year on its annual information return for the IRS (Form 990), the nonprofit must show that it meets this public support test.

Another group of organizations that are considered publicly supported charities are those that normally receive more than one-third of their annual support in any combination of 1) gifts, grants, contributions, or membership fees; and 2) gross receipts from admissions, sales of merchandise, performance of services, or furnishing facilities in an activity that is not an unrelated trade or business.

A last group of nonprofits considered by federal tax law to be publicly supported are *supporting organizations*. These are nonprofits that have established a relationship in support of other public charities and have consequently given up a significant degree of independence, thereby ensuring that they will be responsive to the needs of those other organizations. Qualification in this category is easier because it does not require the organization to satisfy any public support test.

TAX EXEMPTION FOR SOCIAL WELFARE ORGANIZATIONS

Nonprofit organizations that promote social welfare are a separate category of tax-exempt organizations under federal tax law. To qualify for this exempt category, a nonprofit must promote in some way the common good and general welfare of the public in general or people of a community, such as working for civic betterment or social improvements. Promotion of social welfare specifically excludes the operation of a social club for the benefit of members or carrying on business with the general public in a for-profit manner.

A social welfare organization may spend any or all of its funds on attempting to influence legislation that is germane to its social welfare purpose. Because social welfare agencies have unlimited latitude in the amount of legislative activity they can engage in, this is often the category of tax exemption chosen by advocacy groups. In contrast, a public charity must not exceed limits that are designed to restrict to an "insubstantial" amount the funds or efforts that a charity can spend on legislative work.

The concept of social welfare requires that the benefits must affect a whole community of people rather than a private subset of citizens. Benefits conveyed by a social welfare organization that are restricted to a closed member group do not ordinarily have the requisite community benefit to qualify for tax exemption. However, if the benefits are made available to a membership that is open to a cross-section of the community, then the requisite community benefit should be present. The number of persons benefited is not necessarily conclusive under this definition.

Nonprofit organizations may apply for recognition of exemption from federal income tax as a social welfare organization under Section 501(c)(4) by filing a completed Form 1024 with the IRS (available online at www.irs.gov/eo).

CAN TRADE ASSOCIATIONS QUALIFY FOR TAX EXEMPTION?

Trade associations are commonly organized as nonprofit organizations and may qualify for tax exemption under section 501(c)(6) of the Code. To qualify, an organization must meet five tests:

1. It must be an association of persons, companies, or other entities with a common business or professional interest, and its purpose must be to promote that common interest;

2. It must not be organized for profit;

3. No part of its net earnings may inure to the benefit of any private shareholder or individual;

4. Its primary activities must be directed to the improvement of conditions for one or more lines of business or for a profession, rather than providing services or assistance for individual persons or companies; and

5. Its purpose must not be to engage in a regular business of a kind normally carried on for profit, even if the business is operated on a cooperative basis or produces only sufficient income to be self-sustaining.

An organization seeking recognition of its tax-exempt status as a trade association will file an application Form 1024.

A TAX ON UNRELATED INCOME

Under federal tax law, an organization must be organized and operated exclusively for permissible purposes in order to qualify as a tax-exempt charity. However, a charitable organization may carry on an insubstantial level of activity that is not related to its exempt purposes (called *unrelated business activities*). Organizations that are considered tax exempt are nevertheless required to pay taxes on income earned from unrelated business activities. Tax-exempt organizations with an annual gross income of $1,000 or more from an unrelated trade or business must file Form 990-T, Exempt Organization Business Income Tax Return with the IRS, and pay any tax due.

For activities to be considered unrelated, all of the following conditions must be met: 1) The activity must be a trade or business; 2) the trade or business must be regularly carried on by the organization; and 3) the conduct of the trade or business must not be substantially related to the organization's performance of its exempt functions (other than through the production of income).

The phrase "trade or business" is generally defined as any activity carried on for the production of income from the sale of goods or performance of services. An activity does not lose identity as a trade or business merely because it is carried on with other activities that are related to the exempt purposes of an organization. And an activity that constitutes an unrelated trade or business does not have to result in a profit; it can be a money-loser and still maintain its characterization.

Some types of trade or business activities are specifically excluded by federal tax law from the definition of unrelated: 1) a trade or business in which substantially all work is performed for the organization by individuals without compensation, i.e., by volunteers; 2) a trade or business carried on primarily for the convenience of the exempt organization's members, students, patients, officers, or employees; and 3) a trade or business that consists of selling merchandise, substantially all of which has been received by the organization as gifts or contributions.

Since many nonprofits engage in activities that might be considered a regular business, the majority of the IRS rulings on unrelated business income have focused on whether the activities are *substantially* related to the organization's tax-exempt purposes. If they are, then those activities are considered related and the income they generate is not taxable. To make this determination, the IRS examines how close the relationship is between 1) the business activities that generate the income and 2) the accomplishment of the organization's exempt purposes. The production or distribution of goods or the performance of services from which income is derived must contribute importantly to the accomplishment of the organization's exempt purposes for the income to qualify as related. For example, an educational charity may publish and sell books related to its field or a hospital may sell drugs to its patients without incurring the unrelated business income tax.

Certain types of income are excluded from the calculation of unrelated income: All dividends, interest, and annuities, as well as any deductions directly connected with these types of income, are excluded from the calculation of unrelated business taxable income. Royalties (and deductions directly connected with them) are also excluded from unrelated business income. (Royalties do *not* include payment for personal services.) For many years, the IRS took the position that the rental or exchange of an organization's mailing list was not an exempt royalty and therefore produced unrelated business income. But after a number of adverse court cases, the IRS appears to have abandoned this position and most nonprofits now treat this income as exempt royalties.

Rents from *real* property are also excluded from the calculation of unrelated business taxable income. Rents from *personal* property that is leased along with real property are excluded if the amount attributable to the personal property is only an incidental part of the total rent received under the lease. Payments for the use or occupancy of rooms and other space where services are rendered to the occupant (for example, hotel rooms, parking lots, warehouses) do not constitute rent from real property and are not exempt. But payments for the use or occupancy of entire private residences in multiple housing units or offices in any office building are generally treated as rent from real property, if additional services are not provided.

One area of frequent confusion is how to characterize the financial support from for-profit corporate sponsorships that many charitable organizations receive. Not surprisingly, nonprofits often recognize corporate sponsorships or donations by identifying the donors in their external communications. In some cases, this could rise to the level of advertising, which would convert the financial donation into advertising revenue — an unrelated business activity and therefore taxable. In 2002, the IRS published rules setting forth its position on this issue.

Under these rules, if a payment from a for-profit corporation to a charitable organization is a *qualified sponsorship payment*, it does not constitute income from an unrelated trade or business and will not be subject to taxation. A qualified sponsorship payment is any payment of money, transfer of property, or performance of services by a commercial enterprise to a charitable organization with respect to which there is no arrangement or expectation that the for-profit will receive any *substantial return benefit*. (And the sponsored activity does not have to be related to the charitable organization's tax-exempt purpose.) A substantial return benefit is something more than the use or acknowledgment of the name or logo (or product lines) of the for-profit corporation's trade or business in connection with the activities of the exempt organization. A nonprofit wishing to avoid generating unrelated business income from those sponsorships should carefully construct its program in accordance with these rules.

As we've seen, the fact that a nonprofit produces some unrelated business taxable income does not necessarily jeopardize the organization's tax exemption. But how much unrelated business income can an exempt organization generate before its tax exemption is at risk? There is no quantitative answer to this question. Instead, the IRS applies a "reasonably commensurate" test to an exempt organization's unrelated activities: As long as an exempt organization's charitable program is reasonably commensurate with its resources, it will not lose its exemption. If, however, the unrelated business activities become the primary purpose of the organization, its exemption could be revoked by the IRS.

Tax Deductibility of Donations

For most nonprofit organizations, fundraising is the staff of life. Without donor support, their existence would not be sustainable. Acknowledging this truth, and recognizing the valuable public services provided by charitable organizations, federal and state laws provide an extra incentive — in addition to the donor's desire to support the nonprofit's mission — in the form of an income tax deduction to those making contributions to charitable nonprofits. Not surprisingly, if the government is going to forgo substantial revenues in the form of tax deductions, it is going to have a lot to say about how charities may raise those tax-deductible funds and the extent to which individuals may take corresponding deductions.

With few exceptions, individual donors may only take deductions on their individual returns with respect to donations made to charitable organizations, that is, those described in section 501(c)(3) of the Internal Revenue Code. (Because of this, most nonprofits that do not qualify as charitable organizations are not involved in active fundraising. These noncharitable organizations generally rely instead on other sources of revenue for operations, such as income from the furtherance of their tax-exempt purposes, dues, grants, and unrelated business income.)

The IRS primarily regulates charitable fundraising through: 1) charitable gift substantiation rules; 2) *quid pro quo* contribution rules; and 3) rules pertaining to public charity status. (It should also be noted that the U.S. Postal Service and the Federal Trade Commission regulate charitable solicitation with respect to nonprofit mailing rates and telemarketing, respectively.) On the donor side, the IRS likewise prescribes rules with respect to income tax, estate tax, and gift tax deductions for charitable contributions.

The IRS has developed substantiation and disclosure requirements for charitable contributions that are helpfully explained in IRS Publication 1771 (available at www.irs.gov/eo). Under these requirements, there are two general rules to which nonprofit organizations must adhere. First, a charitable nonprofit must provide a written acknowledgment to an individual who makes any single contribution of $250.00 or more. (Otherwise, the donor cannot claim a charitable contribution deduction on his or her federal income tax return.)

Second, a charitable organization must provide a special written acknowledgment to a donor who receives goods or services from the charity in exchange for a single payment that exceeds $75.00. These are called *quid pro quo* contributions, that is, contributions for which the organization returns some benefit to the giver. If a charitable organization provides goods or services to an individual in exchange for a contribution of $75.00 or more, the organization's written acknowledgment must describe the goods or services and must provide an estimate of their fair-market value. The donor's tax deduction is then limited to the difference between the amount of his or her contribution and the fair market value of the goods and services that he or she received.

There are certain exceptions to the *quid pro quo* rule. First, if the goods or services provided by the charity in exchange for a contribution are insubstantial, their value does not have to be offset against the donation. The IRS defines goods and services as insubstantial if one of the following is applicable:

1. The fair market value of the benefits received does not exceed the lesser of 2 percent of the donation or $82.00; or

2. The donation is at least $41.00; the only items that the charity provides the donor contain the organization's name or logo on them (calendars, mugs, posters, hats, newsletters); and the items cost the nonprofit $8.20 or less. (These amounts are indexed and adjusted periodically by the IRS for inflation.)

Another exception is when an annual member benefit is provided in exchange for a payment of $75.00 or less and the membership benefit consists only of recurring rights, such as free and discounted admissions to the charity's facilities and events; discounts on purchases made from the charity's gift shop; or free or discounted admission to member-only events that the nonprofit sponsors, where the per-person cost (exclusive of overhead) is within the low-cost limit. For example, a charity may offer a $60.00 annual membership that entitles the member to free admission to the organization's planned events, plus a book worth $20.00. The organization's written acknowledgment to the individual would state only that it is providing the donor an item of value worth $20.00 (since the free admission to the organization's events would be considered insubstantial and would be disregarded in figuring valuation).

A further exception applies to religious charities: If a religious organization provides only *intangible religious benefits* to a donor, the acknowledgment to the donor does not need to describe or value these benefits, but rather can simply state that the organization provided intangible religious benefits to the donor. Benefits that qualify as intangible religious benefits are those that are provided by the charity exclusively for religious purposes and which are not normally sold in commercial transactions outside of a gift context. These might include admission to a religious ceremony or the wine used in a religious service. Benefits that the IRS does not consider intangible religious benefits would include education leading to a recognized degree, travel services, or consumer goods.

Although noncharitable nonprofits, such as social welfare organizations or trade associations, do not qualify for tax-deductible contributions, the disclosure rules apply to noncharitable nonprofit organizations as well (unless the organization's gross annual receipts are not normally in excess of $100,000). A fundraising solicitation by or on behalf of a noncharitable organization is required to contain an express statement, in a conspicuous and easily recognizable format, that gifts made to the organization may not be deducted as charitable contributions for federal income tax purposes. Letters or telephone calls that are not part of a coordinated campaign that solicits more than 10 persons within a calendar year are excluded from these rules. If an organization fails to abide by the disclosure requirement, it is subject to a penalty of $1,000 per day with a maximum of $10,000 per year, unless reasonable cause for the failure to meet the requirements is shown. Intentional disregard of the rules increases the penalties substantially.

COMPLYING WITH SUBSTANTIATION AND DISCLOSURE REQUIREMENTS

Charities can best observe substantiation and disclosure requirements by providing acknowledgments that include both the name of the organization and the amount of the contribution, and, when appropriate:

- a description of any noncash contributions;

- a statement that no goods or services were provided by the charity in return for the contribution (if this applies);

- a description and good-faith estimate of the value of any goods or services provided by the charity to the donor in return for a gift; and

- a statement, if applicable, that goods or services provided in return for the contribution consisted entirely of intangible religious benefits.

The IRS does not require that a donor's Social Security number or tax identification number be included in a written acknowledgment to the donor. Nor does the IRS require any specific form for the acknowledgments. The agency has indicated that letters and postcards or computer-generated forms with the appropriate information are acceptable. The acknowledgment can also be provided electronically by e-mail to the donor. Charitable organizations should send the required written acknowledgment to donors by January 31 following the year of the donation. In order to be considered contemporaneous with the contribution, the donor must receive the acknowledgment by the date on which he or she files a tax return for the year of the contribution.

The IRS has suggested the following as examples of acceptable written acknowledgments:

- "Thank you for your cash contribution of $300.00 that (name of organization) received on December 12, 2004. No goods or services were provided in exchange for your contribution."

- "Thank you for your cash contribution of $350.00 that (name of organization) received on May 6, 2005. In exchange for your contribution, we gave you a cookbook with an estimated fair market value of $60.00."

The statement must be furnished with either the solicitation or the acknowledgment of the contribution. It must be in writing and in a manner that must come to the donor's attention. Thus, disclosures in small print within a larger document may be inadequate to satisfy this requirement. Penalties apply to charities that do not satisfy the written disclosure requirement. The penalty is $10.00 per contribution, not to exceed $5,000 per fundraising event or per mailing. A charity can avoid the penalty if it can show a failure to meet the requirement was due to reasonable cause.

STATE REGISTRATION AND DISCLOSURE

States generally follow the tax-deductibility rules of the federal government. Their primary focus is on ensuring that charities accurately represent to the public their operations and the purposes for which they are soliciting funds so that unscrupulous organizations and individuals do not take funds from the public in an improper or deceptive manner. This is generally the province of the state attorney general, whose job description includes protecting consumers within the state.

The vast majority of states require registration and disclosure of fundraising methods and operations by any charitable organization that solicits funds within their borders. While there are some common approaches taken by states to the regulation of charitable solicitation — and a number of states have adopted a uniform registration form — each state has its own process and regulations. A discussion of each state's regulation scheme is beyond the scope of this chapter. However, it is important for charities soliciting in more than one state to understand the rules that apply to them and to register with and report to states as required by their laws. Most states now do a good job of providing the appropriate information on the Web site of the state attorney general's office.

PUBLIC DISCLOSURE OF TAX INFORMATION

In 1999, the IRS published final regulations requiring public disclosure of information relating to operations, revenues, expenses, and personnel of most tax-exempt organizations. All organizations must have in place a process for releasing to the public the information required by the regulations.

A nonprofit should carefully adhere to the process stipulated by the IRS for making available for public inspection the nonprofit's application for tax exemption and its annual information returns (Form 990), and for supplying copies of that material to individuals or organizations requesting them. The IRS rules set forth the place and time that the organization must make this information available; the conditions that may be placed on requests for copies; and the amount, form, and time of payment of any fees that are charged for the information by the organization. They also make special provision for those organizations making the information widely available by posting it on the Internet. (To protect charities from harassment campaigns, the rules also establish standards for handling cases involving multiple requests of copies.)

Failure of an organization to comply with these rules will result in financial penalties being imposed by the IRS — as well as a guaranteed public relations black eye for the nonprofit! If the failure to comply involves the Form 990, the organization is subject to a $20-per-day penalty (with a maximum of $10,000 for any one return). If the compliance failure is with regard to the organization's application for tax exemption, it is subject to a penalty of $20 per day (with no maximum). If the IRS finds that the organization *willfully* fails to comply with the disclosure requirements, it is subject to an additional penalty of $5,000 for each annual information return or tax-exemption application involved.

SANCTIONS AGAINST PRIVATE INUREMENT

Until recently, a charity's violation of the private inurement proscription presented a difficult choice for the IRS: Let the nonprofit go scot-free or club it with the only penalty available to the IRS — revocation of tax-exempt status. That changed in 1996 when Congress amended the Internal Revenue Code to permit *intermediate sanctions* for some violations. (They are "intermediate" in that they lie between taking no action and revoking an organization's tax exemption.)

The intermediate sanctions are aimed at curbing financial transactions between a tax-exempt organization and "insiders" — persons who can exert substantial influence over the organization when the transaction results in an excessive benefit to such individuals. The IRS rules implementing the law impose tax sanctions on individuals who benefit from an excess benefit transaction and on nonprofit managers who participate in such a transaction, knowing that it was improper. The rules apply to public charities (charitable organizations other than private foundations) and social welfare organizations; these entities are termed, for this purpose, *applicable tax-exempt organizations.*

An excess benefit transaction is one in which an economic benefit is provided by an applicable tax-exempt nonprofit directly or indirectly to a *disqualified* person, if the value of the economic benefit provided by the nonprofit exceeds the value of the consideration (including the performance of services) received for providing the benefit. In other words, was the disqualified person's compensation from the nonprofit for goods or services excessive and unreasonable? Or was the financial transaction based on the fair market value of a similar service or a product?

First, what is a disqualified person? The IRS defines the term as: 1) any individual who was, at any time during the five-year period ending on the date of the transaction involved, in a position to exercise substantial influence over the affairs of the organization (whether by virtue of being an organization manager or otherwise); 2) a member of the family of an individual described in the preceding category; and 3) an entity in which persons described in the preceding two categories own more than 35 percent of an interest. An organization manager is a trustee, director, or officer of the organization, as well as an individual having powers or responsibilities similar to those of trustees, directors, or officers of the organization — which could include senior executives.

How do you determine if compensation provided to or a financial arrangement (such as a loan) transacted with a disqualified person is reasonable and not excessive? The IRS says there is a presumption of reasonableness, which arises when a compensation or financial arrangement with a disqualified person is approved by an independent board (or an independent committee authorized by the board) 1) that is composed entirely of individuals unrelated to and not subject to the control of the disqualified person(s) involved in the arrangement; 2) that obtained and relied upon appropriate data as to comparability; and 3) that adequately documented the basis for its determination of reasonableness. (For example, the record included an evaluation of the individual whose compensation was being established and the basis for determining that the individual's compensation was reasonable in light of that evaluation and data). If these three criteria are satisfied, the presumption of reasonableness can only be rebutted if the IRS develops sufficient contrary evidence to counter the evidence put forth by the parties to the transaction.

The penalties for excess benefit transactions can be severe: A disqualified person whom the IRS finds has benefited from an excess benefit transaction must first repay the excess benefit to the nonprofit, and then is subject to an initial tax equal to 25 percent of the amount of the excess benefit. (An additional tax equivalent to 200 percent of the excess benefit may be imposed on a disqualified person if the transaction is not corrected within a specified period of time.) An organization manager who participated in an excess benefit transaction, knowing that it was such a transaction, is subject to an initial tax of 10 percent of the excess benefit (subject to a maximum of $10,000), if an initial tax is also imposed on a disqualified person.

In general, intermediate sanctions are the only penalties the IRS will impose for excess benefit transactions, unless the excess benefit rises to a level where it calls into question whether, on the whole, the organization truly functions as a charitable or social welfare organization and therefore should lose its tax-exempt status.

Tax-exempt status is virtually always sought by nonprofit organizations. Freedom from federal and state income taxation provides nonprofit organizations with the financial foundation they need to carry out their missions. However, tax-exempt status is not a one-size-fits-all proposition. During the organizational and planning phase of the nonprofit organization, the initial board of directors and its consultants will need to carefully consider the most favorable tax-exempt status for which the organization is able to qualify. The founder will want to work in partnership with the organization's counsel and accountants to prepare an effective application for tax-exempt status that will appropriately convey the character, purposes, and operation of the organization in a document that will not only be considered by the Internal Revenue Service, but also by the public. Once tax-exempt status has been recognized by the IRS, the answers provided in the application will set the parameters for the organization's operations. Moreover, obtaining tax-exempt status is only the beginning. The board of directors will need to ensure that the organization maintains compliance with the ever-changing guidelines of the IRS. Emerging trends in governance and transparency in public disclosure warrant the board's oversight of the organization's Form 990 filing as well. The board should be informed about the information contained in this public record document, which includes their names and the address of the organization, the compensation of senior management and key employees, and key financial data regarding the organization. Tax-exempt status for a nonprofit organization affects far more than its obligation to pay taxes. IRS rules and court decisions in this area regulate the core operations of a nonprofit organization, including the composition of its board, its conflict-of-interest policy, and the manner in which its directors discharge their fiduciary duties. Accordingly, careful and ongoing attention to this area of the law is essential.

QUESTIONS THE BOARD SHOULD ASK

- Do we clearly understand the IRS and state rights and restrictions for our tax-exempt and corporate status?

- Have we recently reviewed our gift-acceptance policy and our solicitation practices?

- Are we securing the presumption of reasonableness when we transact with interested directors?

3.
Directors and Officers: On Behalf of the Board

Steven R. Smith

Over the last several years, allegations of corruption and self-dealing at a number of high-profile corporations have led to increased scrutiny of the boards of directors of for-profit companies by government regulators, Wall Street, and investors. Laws passed as a result of these scandals have highlighted the role that for-profit directors must play in the oversight of their companies.

This increased scrutiny is now beginning to extend to nonprofit corporations and their boards. While a board of directors is not involved in the day-to-day operations of the corporation, members of a board — collectively and individually — do have important duties and obligations concerning the business of the corporation. The failure to perform those duties can result in liability to the board of directors or to individual members. So liability and protection against liability are important subjects for any board member to understand.

This is not a reference to the liability of the corporation itself, which can, of course be sued. Corporations suffer from lawsuits every day without the directors of the corporation being sued or being held liable for the actions of the corporation. Generally, when a corporation acts in accordance with its corporate purposes and pursuant to any required authorization by the board of directors, liability resulting from that action will rest with the corporation, not the board.

Liability for board members themselves arises when a director of a nonprofit corporation performs an act that breaches a duty that the director owes to the organization (or fails to perform that necessary duty). Understanding what those duties are and how they are best fulfilled is a prerequisite to service on a board.

The two primary duties that a director owes to a corporation are the duty of due care and the duty of loyalty. Below we will explore these duties, the concept of indemnification of directors for liability incurred as a result of their service as directors, and insurance coverage for directors.

BOARD MEMBERS' LEGAL OBLIGATIONS

THE DUTY OF DUE CARE

The duty of due care (often called simply the *duty of care*) requires that a director perform his or her responsibilities as a board member in good faith and with the care that an ordinarily prudent person *in a like position* would use under similar circumstances. The italicized language is important because it indicates that this duty is not stagnant; it varies as the status and position of the corporation itself varies. For example, the obligations of a director of a nonprofit corporation that is in excellent financial condition and has never experienced any internal malfeasance are quite different from the obligations of a director of a nonprofit in financial distress, or one that has had allegations of fraud and self-dealing against it. The legal duty is the same: again, to act in good faith and with the care that an ordinarily prudent person *in a like position* would use under similar circumstances. What is different are the respective positions and circumstances of the two corporations; those different factual positions and circumstances require special levels of inquiry and involvement in order for a director to satisfy this duty.

Other important aspects of the directors' due care duty include:

- **Adopting policies and procedures that provide for effective oversight of management.** The board delegates the day-to-day responsibility to manage the corporation to a chief executive and the subordinates he hires. But the directors must ensure that procedures are in place that will keep them informed about the position and circumstances of the corporation in order to meet the due care duty.

- **Attending board and committee meetings to which they are assigned so that they will have an opportunity to obtain the information necessary to make an informed judgment about matters on which they must make decisions on behalf of the corporation.** If, as stated above, policies are in place requiring management to provide the board with the quantity and quality of information needed by the board to make reasonably informed decisions, then the duty of due care recognizes that the directors are entitled to rely on that information, those opinions, and other reports prepared by certain persons — so long as the directors reasonably believe the person or committee generating the information is competent to do so. The types of persons directors are entitled to rely on include officers or employees of the corporation, lawyers, CPAs, or a committee of the board on which the director does not serve, as to matters within its authority.

The right to rely on information from others is subject to the condition that the director must reasonably believe the person or committee delivering the information is competent or merits confidence. If a director is not consistently present at meetings then he leaves himself open to a challenge as to whether he has any basis to form a reasonable belief that the person or committee upon whom he relies in making decisions is competent or merits confidence.

Similarly, a director does not act in good faith if he has knowledge that his reliance on information provided by others is not warranted. If the advice of management, a consultant, or a committee of the board has consistently been proven to be wrong in the past, then a director should at least make inquiry into the basis upon which future recommendations from those persons or committees are made.

Another aspect of being adequately informed is asking questions and raising legitimate inquiries. If a director has a concern about a proposed course of action but fails to voice that concern (and ensure that it is recorded in the minutes of the meeting), the law assumes that he assented to any action that was taken on that matter. If a director disagrees with a proposed action before the board, he needs to voice that disagreement and either vote against the action or, if appropriate, abstain from voting.

It is crucial for their own protection that directors ensure that minutes of board meetings are recorded and maintained, so that the actions of each of them are properly memorialized. The minutes should include a record of the discussion of reports received from management and others, discussion surrounding any proposed actions, and any decisions taken by the board, including the votes of each director on those decisions.

- **Acting in an independent manner and exercising independent judgment in matters affecting the nonprofit.** It is inevitable that, in any mix of individuals serving on a board, some directors will have greater knowledge of certain issues than others; or, the personalities of some directors may be more dominant than others. Notwithstanding that, each director is elected or appointed to be a member of the board for his or her own abilities. No director should refrain from voicing objections or asking questions about an issue because another board member has greater knowledge of the subject or is an intimidating personality. A good maxim for directors to follow is: "The only bad question is one that is not asked."

- **Ensuring that the nonprofit acts in accordance with its exempt purposes.** Nonprofit corporations are organized for charitable, religious, social, or other purposes and are granted exemption from federal and state taxation in recognition of the benefits to society resulting from achieving those purposes. Part of the due care duty of a director is to keep the corporation focused on its nonprofit purposes, as outlined in the organization's articles of incorporation and bylaws. In addition to being informed as to the substance of the matters brought before them for decisions, directors must also consider whether the accomplishment of those decisions by the nonprofit will further the exempt purposes of the corporation.

THE DUTY OF LOYALTY

The duty of loyalty requires that a director always act in a manner he believes to be in the best interests of the corporation. Each director's actions must be for the benefit of the nonprofit corporation, not himself. This requires that a director not usurp for himself business opportunities of the nonprofit, that he refrain from conflicts of interest, and that he keep the business of the corporation confidential (except where the information is public knowledge or the board consents to disclosure).

The best guarantee to ensure that directors act in the interests of the corporation is for the nonprofit to have in place a comprehensive conflicts-of-interest policy that:

1. Identifies those persons who are in significant positions of authority and who will be subject to the policy including, at a minimum, the members of the board of directors and all members of senior management (each of whom is in a position to influence how and by whom the business of the corporation is conducted).

2. Identifies the potential interests held by those persons that pose a potential conflict of interest. (Competing interests may include a director's own personal interests, those of his political or business allies or, in certain cases, those of the body that appointed him to the position of director.)

3. Requires the disclosure of the actual or potential conflict to the board of directors. (The corporation, through the board of directors, is entitled to know

what underlying financial or other interests a director or officer may have in a matter being considered by the board.)

4. Provides a process by which a determination is made as to whether a conflict exists and how to deal with that conflict. (If a director has an interest in the matter under consideration, the board may still determine that the best interests of the corporation will be served by working with that director — but the disclosure must be made in the first place so that the line between a benefit to the director and the best interests of the corporation can be determined, and the potential for abuse assessed.)

5. Establishes a process to handle violations of the policy.

6. Adheres to and consistently applies the adopted policy to all board members.

The Internal Revenue Service has published a sample conflicts-of-interest policy in its Continuing Professional Education materials and in its newly revised form 1023 (available online at www.irs.gov/eo). While directed at health care organizations, this model policy is an excellent resource for all nonprofits. The IRS states in the model policy that the adoption of a substantial conflicts-of-interest policy is a factor in demonstrating that the corporation is being operated for the benefit of the community, rather than for the benefit of individuals. (For further information regarding conflicts-of-interest policies, see Suggested Resources on page 135.)

OFFICERS' DUTIES

Directors who are also officers may have additional duty imposed on them. In general, officers do not have a different or higher duty imposed on them than for other members of the board. However, in the course of carrying out his or her responsibilities as an officer, an officer-director may receive information or be involved in activities to which other directors are not privy. In this case, in order to satisfy the director's duties of due care and loyalty, the officer-director may need to exercise greater caution or maintain confidentiality at a level not required of the other directors. An officer with access to more information than other directors must take account of that extra information when meeting his duty to act with the care of an ordinarily prudent person *in a like position.*

ARE THEY SET IN STONE?

In certain instances, the duties of nonprofit directors may change. For example, when a nonprofit becomes insolvent, or approaches insolvency, it is generally recognized that there is a shift in the duty of directors. (At what point a corporation is deemed insolvent is determined by each state's law.) In this case, the directors now owe a duty not only to the corporation, but also to the wider scope of the corporation's business interests — most notably the creditors of the corporation. The reason the law shifts a director's duty in this instance is that, once the corporation becomes insolvent, the creditors may be the only parties "left standing" that have a continuing business interest in the assets of the corporation.

This shift highlights the importance for continuing board members to be informed about the financial circumstances of the corporation. Members of the board cannot simply view the corporation as a failed enterprise, walk away from it, and not be concerned about the ultimate disposition of the corporation and its assets. Creditors have dealt with the corporation with the understanding that it is acting in good faith and conducting its business in a responsible manner. Conducting business responsibly means being concerned about the debtors of the nonprofit and about repaying debts that have been properly incurred on behalf of the corporation.

WHAT ARE DIRECTORS LIABLE FOR?

One of the most important concerns for nonprofit directors is the liability they may incur when serving as directors — and the important protections that the law provides them in the case of a lawsuit. The most crucial protection is this: If the directors of a corporation comply with the duties imposed on them, they will generally not be liable for the decisions they make on behalf of the corporation — even if it is later determined that a particular decision was unwise or erroneous.

Under what is known as the *business judgment rule*, directors cannot be held liable for losses resulting to the corporation as a result of errors in their judgment if they acted in good faith and with due care to their responsibilities to the corporation. (The business judgment protection does not apply when it is shown that a director has benefited personally from a decision.)

Further, the business judgment rule provides a presumption that directors have acted in accordance with their respective duties. This means anyone challenging the directors' actions has the burden of proof to affirmatively demonstrate that the directors did not satisfy their duty to the corporation and that the failure to do so resulted in harm to the corporation or to the complainant. (Some states go further and provide immunity from liability to directors for their actions if they simply acted in good faith — and as long as they do not receive compensation for their services to the nonprofit.)

The effect of the business judgment rule is to allow directors to act on behalf of the corporation without fear of being held liable for making a wrong or unwise business decision — as long as the director acted in good faith, after exercising due care, and in the reasonable belief that the action taken was in the best interests of the corporation.

Notwithstanding the protections of the business judgment rule, it is possible for directors to be liable in an individual capacity for their actions as directors. If a director acts in bad faith or commits fraud or a criminal act while serving on a board, that director may be held individually liable, both civilly and criminally. For example, in some states loans to directors by a nonprofit organization are prohibited; if a director votes in favor of a loan from a nonprofit organization to another director in violation of this law, the director may be individually liable for repayment of the loan to the nonprofit. Another example of personal liability is found in the discussion of intermediate sanctions in Chapter 2. These rules, designed to penalize individuals who improperly benefit from transactions with charitable organizations, impose a penalty tax of up to $10,000 on individual directors who knowingly and willfully approve transactions that excessively benefit individuals.

INDEMNIFICATION OF DIRECTORS

The law, of course, does not prohibit or protect a director from being sued, but it does provide significant protection for him if he is. Most states have statutes that either authorize or require that a director be reimbursed for expenses related to defending himself in a lawsuit based on his actions on the board of directors. Generally, those statutes provide that, where a director acted in good faith in the reasonable belief that his actions were in the best interests of the corporation, and fully prevails in a suit against him involving his duties as a director, then the corporation is required to reimburse him for his expenses (including attorneys' fees). Indemnification is generally prohibited if a legal proceeding results in a judgment that the director acted in his own or others' interests and not in the best interests of the corporation.

Some state statutes provide for a director to be advanced attorneys' fees and other expenses in certain instances. Others require that, prior to any indemnification being paid to a director, the director must apply to the board for that relief and that a majority of the disinterested directors on the board must authorize the indemnification.

Indemnification rights generally arise from three sources: statutes, corporate organizational documents, and insurance. State statutes are just the starting point for indemnification rights because most state laws provide that the articles of incorporation or bylaws of the corporation may expand a director's indemnification rights (although some limit the rights extended to those in the state's statute). Therefore, a director's right to indemnification can be significantly broadened by those documents. Directors should take care that the nonprofit's corporate documents provide indemnification rights at least as comprehensive as those under applicable state law.

INSURANCE AS PROTECTION

When a director is sued for actions he has taken in his capacity as a director of the corporation, he expects to be protected from personally paying the expenses to defend the lawsuit and from having to pay the cost of any judgment against him. Although statutes and a nonprofit's organizational documents will provide for a director to be indemnified, not all nonprofits will have the financial resources necessary to fund the expense of protracted litigation or of a resulting adverse judgment. For this and other reasons, nonprofits usually purchase directors' and officers' (D&O) liability insurance.

D&O insurance is obtained by a nonprofit organization primarily for the purpose of protecting directors from personal liability resulting from their good-faith actions in the course of their duties. This type of coverage has become quite common in the nonprofit world and many prospective directors will understandably decline to serve unless they receive such coverage. Coverage may be provided directly to the director, or if the organization is indemnifying the director, the coverage may be in the form of reimbursement to the organization for its expenses. Typically, coverage will extend for claims of breach of various federal and state laws, including employment laws, common-law court claims such as slander and libel, and more recently, for claims under the IRS's intermediate sanctions rules for excess benefit transactions approved by directors.

D&O insurance protects both the board members and the organization itself: It protects the directors by providing a source of funds for indemnification that is not dependent on the financial wherewithal or stability of the corporation; it protects the corporation by shifting the financial burden of litigation and any adverse judgment to an insurance company. Just as important, many persons will understandably be reluctant to serve on a board unless the nonprofit carries D&O insurance. Without such insurance, a nonprofit may lose the services of many talented and valuable persons for its board.

Because D&O insurance is so important to the nonprofit and its board, directors and managers should carefully compare policies and, in particular, take note of any exclusions from coverage in the policy. (If a policy excludes areas of coverage that are important to a nonprofit, often a D&O provider will agree to cover those areas through a policy "rider" — for an additional cost.)

The following steps should be taken to secure this important D&O coverage:

- The nonprofit's management should retain the services of a knowledgable insurance broker who can ensure that the proper coverage is provided at the most affordable rate. Most policies will contain a deductible amount — the higher the deductible, the lower the policy's premium — but any deductible should be paid by the corporation, not the director. Competitive bidding for a policy should be entertained whenever possible.

- Directors should review the coverage and terms with management and should ask questions regarding the proposed policy. Importantly, this review should include the nonprofit's *application* for coverage since the representations made in the application will be relied on by the insurance company when agreeing to provide the coverage and the nonprofit is usually bound by the statements it makes in its initial application.

- The company chosen to provide the coverage should be highly rated by insurance rating agencies. It does no good to buy a policy if the insurance company is not around to pay the claim.

- The policy should require the insurance company to provide the corporation and its directors with a defense to any lawsuit and to pay for that defense.

- Careful attention should be paid to the notice provisions of the policy since the failure to comply with required notice to the insurance company of a potential or pending lawsuit may, in some instances, invalidate the coverage.

Note: These same steps can be followed to ensure that a nonprofit organization also has the other two types of insurance that a nonprofit of any size should, at a minimum, have in force to protect its assets and stability: a general commercial liability policy and a media perils "errors & omissions" liability policy.

Chapter Q&As

Q: Can I be sued individually for my actions when I serve as a director of a nonprofit organization?

A: Yes. Under the U.S. system of jurisprudence, individual board members can be sued, in addition to the organization itself, for claims related to their duties on behalf of the organization. For the most part, if a director acts in good faith and properly discharges his fiduciary duties, he will be protected from liability under common-law doctrines such as the business judgment rule, and in many cases, under state statutory law. In addition, many nonprofit organizations will indemnify directors for any individual liability that may be incurred in the scope of their duties. Directors' and officers' liability insurance may provide coverage for these claims as well. However, if a director acts in bad faith, with gross negligence, or knowingly in violation of law, he will likely not escape personal liability for damages, fines, penalty taxes, or other claims.

Q: What is D&O insurance? Do we need it?

A: A directors' and officers' (D&O) insurance policy is obtained by an organization for the purpose of protecting board members and officers from personal liability resulting from their good-faith actions in the course of their duties. This type of coverage has become quite common in the nonprofit world and many prospective directors will decline to serve unless they receive such coverage. Coverage may be provided directly to the director, or if the organization is indemnifying the director, the coverage may be in the form of reimbursement to the organization for its expenses. Typically, coverage will extend for claims of breach of various federal and state laws, including employment laws, common-law court claims such as slander and libel, and more recently, for claims under the IRS's intermediate sanctions rules for excess benefit transactions approved by directors.

The issue of the fiduciary duties of directors of a nonprofit organization is getting heightened attention by a growing array of regulators, legislators, and commentators. More than ever, directors must have a strong working knowledge of what it means to exercise their duties of care, loyalty, and obedience. A board of directors must have good "I's" for the demands of these duties; that is, it must be **involved** with the organization's governance, **informed** about the matters before it, and show **integrity** in making the decisions required of it. Directors should be wary of oversight by state attorneys general, the IRS, charity watchdog groups, and others regarding the manner in which they have governed the organization. Timely and effective self-evaluation by the board will go a long way towards ensuring that directors are following best practices and operating in the most efficient and effective manner possible. The chief executive should carefully consider the availability and scope of directors' and officers' liability insurance coverage and work with the board to obtain an appropriate policy. Both the chief executive and the board should discuss and understand the extent to which individual directors could have personal liability for actions of the organization, and the means available for minimizing that liability and indemnifying directors for their good-faith actions on behalf of the organization.

Questions the Board Should Ask

- Do we regularly educate our board members about their legal duties and liabilities as the fiduciaries for our organization?

- Do our minutes accurately convey what happened in the board meeting?

- Do we have a clear conflict-of-interest policy, and is it firmly enforced?

- Is our D&O liability insurance coverage adequate?

4.
Lobbying and Electioneering

David B. Hamilton

Nonprofit organizations frequently want to — and do — engage in political activities. But federal tax laws restrict and regulate what is permissible political activity, and what is not. The restrictions in federal tax law are very important to nonprofits because of the potential penalties for violating them: taxes, fines, and, ultimately, revocation of tax-exempt status.

Federal law divides political activity into two types: Actions designed to influence or affect legislation ("lobbying") are permissible for public charities within limits; actions that affect elections ("electioneering") are never permissible for public charities. However, the law allows considerably more leeway in these activities to social welfare organizations, trade associations, and Section 527 political organizations, than it does to public charities.

Since public charities are the most numerous nonprofits and are subject to the most restrictive limits, they are at the forefront of the discussion that follows.

CHARITABLE NONPROFITS' LOBBYING ACTIVITIES

In general, tax-exempt public charities — those described in Section 501(c)(3) of the Internal Revenue Code — may address issues of public policy without the activity being treated as lobbying. A charity may hold educational meetings, prepare and distribute educational materials, or otherwise examine public policy issues in an educational manner — that is, addressing the full range of issues and arguments — without fear of having these activities or communications classified as lobbying.

Charitable organizations are permitted to go even further and attempt to influence legislation, i.e., lobby, as long as it is not a "substantial part" of their overall tax-exempt activities. To determine whether an organization's lobbying is a substantial part or not, each charity is allowed to choose between one of two tests:

1. *The substantial part test:* If a charity chooses this test, it relies on a general and undefined standard that "no substantial part" of a charitable organization's activities may constitute carrying on propaganda or otherwise attempting to influence legislation. There is no bright line when assessing whether the substantial limit has been exceeded. Instead, the IRS will look at various facts, including the amount of time devoted to lobbying by employees and volunteers, and the amount of funds expended by the organization on the activity at issue. If the IRS determines that a charity has exceeded the substantial limit, its tax-exempt status may be revoked.

2. *The expenditures test:* This test allows a charity elect to have its lobbying restricted to specific dollar limits that are scaled to the total expenditures of the nonprofit. The test, also known by its Internal Revenue Code section as the "501(h) election," can permit up to a maximum annual lobbying expenditure of $1,000,000. If the organization exceeds its lobbying expenditure limit in a

given year, it is subject to an excise tax equal to 25 percent of the excess expenditure. If it exceeds its limit over a four-year period, it may have its tax-exempt status revoked, making all of its income for that period taxable.

Exactly what is meant by "influencing legislation"? The term *legislation* includes an action by the U.S. Congress; by any state legislature; by any city or county council or similar governing body; or by the public in a referendum, ballot initiative, or constitutional amendment. But — most notably — it generally does *not* include actions by executive, judicial, or administrative bodies or employees. So trying to influence regulations being written by an executive agency to implement a law or challenging a law in court usually falls outside the scope of lobbying. (But attempting to influence an executive branch official to take a position on pending legislation does fall within the definition of lobbying.)

Is all contact or communication with a legislative body considered lobbying? Not unless it refers to and reflects a view on specific legislation. Therefore, the IRS has stated that the following types of communication do not fall within the definition of lobbying:

1. Making available to legislators and the public the results of nonpartisan analysis, study, or research;

2. Examining and discussing broad social, economic, and similar problems;

3. Providing technical advice or assistance to a governmental body or to a legislative committee in response to a written request by such body; or

4. Communicating with a government official or employee, other than a communication with a member or employee of a legislative body when the communication would otherwise constitute the influencing of legislation, or a communication with the principal purpose of influencing legislation.

Attempting to influence legislation not only covers communication with any member or employee of a legislative body or with any government official who may participate in the formulation of legislation (called "direct" lobbying), it also includes trying to affect the opinions of the general public or any segment of it on legislation (known as "grass-roots" lobbying). The distinction is important because the Section 501(h) test requires a charity to observe separate maximum limits for direct and for grass-roots lobbying. To qualify as grass-roots lobbying, a communication to the general public must: 1) refer to specific legislation; 2) reflect a view or opinion on that legislation; and 3) include a call to action encouraging the recipient to contact a legislator or legislative body.

Communications between an organization and its *bona fide* members with respect to legislation of interest to the organization and its members are excluded from the definition of grass-roots lobbying. But if the charity's communication includes a call to action that directly encourages its members to contact legislators to influence specific legislation or encourages its members to urge nonmembers to influence legislation, then it is classified as grass-roots lobbying.

Finally, the law recognizes an exemption from the definition of lobbying for the self-preservation or self-interest of a charity. Therefore, communicating with a legislator or legislative body with respect to a decision that might affect the existence of the organization, its powers and duties, its tax-exempt status, or the deduction of contributions to the organization is expressly excluded from being treated as lobbying under the Code.

Before embarking on lobbying activities, a charity should be sure that it is administratively equipped to handle the significant record-keeping that is required. For example, the organization must be able to track not only the time and expenses of its staff in communicating with a lawmaker, but the time they take to prepare for the contact, and the time spent researching and writing the communications. Additionally, any direct costs such as printing or photocopying must also be included in lobbying expenses.

Lobbying expenditures are reported to the IRS each year on the annual information federal return Form 990 (by charities following the expenditure test). But in addition, many legislative bodies require filing of separate reports with them, in an effort to promote disclosure to the public of expenditures by persons and groups attempting to influence the lawmaking process. Most notably, the U.S. Congress, through the Lobbying Disclosure Act, requires detailed semiannual reports. Many state legislatures and even city and county councils also have reporting requirements of which nonprofits need to be cognizant.

ELECTIONEERING BY PUBLIC CHARITIES

The prohibition in federal tax law against public charities engaging in any activities that affect an election is an *absolute* prohibition. There is no substantial-part-of-a-charity's-activities test as there is for lobbying by a charity. The public policy reason for this total prohibition is the desire to keep donations, given by donors in support of charitable public purposes, from being siphoned off into partisan electioneering activities. And, just as important, because a charity's donors are often given a government tax deduction, the prohibition prevents what is tantamount to public tax dollars from being used to influence elections.

The IRS has noted that intervention in an electoral campaign by a charitable organization may be subtle or blatant. It may seem to be justified by the press of events. It may even be inadvertent. None of this is relevant. The law prohibits all forms of participation or intervention in any election campaign, regardless of intent. An organization can violate the proscription even if it acts for reasons other than wishing to intervene in an election campaign. Further, in the IRS's view, having a nonpartisan motivation is irrelevant when determining whether the electioneering prohibition has been violated by a charity. Electioneering has been found by the IRS when an otherwise educational activity influenced voter preferences, even if the organization's motives were nonpartisan. An educational or nonpartisan motive is no defense to a violation.

The ultimate penalty for violating the electioneering prohibition is harsh: loss of tax exemption for the organization. In addition, the IRS may impose an excise tax on impermissible electioneering expenditures by the organization. In cases where the violation is minor relative to the overall program of charitable activities carried on by the organization, the IRS has a tendency to assess only the excise tax, while leaving the organization's tax exemption intact.

What Is Included in the Definition of Electioneering?

In general, a public charity may not oppose, endorse, work for, or otherwise support a candidate seeking election to any public office at any level (federal, state, or local). No funds, facilities, personnel, or resources of a charity may be used to support or oppose a candidate. Even intangible assets, such as the goodwill of a charity, may not be utilized in an electoral campaign. Additionally, a charity must take care that any coalition or association of organizations to which it belongs does not engage in electioneering activities. Public charities also may *not* establish or support a political action committee (PAC).

While many activities can clearly and easily be identified as partisan electioneering, others may not be so black and white. In those cases, a determination is made by the IRS by looking at all the facts and circumstances of the suspect activity. The agency will look not only at the activity itself, but also at the consequences of the activity.

For example, the following activities by a charitable organization would clearly fall under the definition of electioneering — and therefore be prohibited:

- Publishing or distributing written statements, or making oral statements, on behalf of or in opposition to any candidate for any federal, state, or local office.

- Distributing partisan campaign literature.

- Providing financial or in-kind support (e.g., use of volunteers, paid staff, equipment, mailing lists) to a candidate for any federal, state, or local office.

- Establishing or supporting (financial or in-kind) a political action committee.

But the following activities *may or may not* act to influence an election, depending upon the facts and circumstances:

- Inviting a candidate to make an appearance at a charitable organization's event.

- Sponsoring candidate forums or distributing voter guides that evidence a bias in favor of or against the way candidates have voted on legislation.

- Using issue advocacy in fundraising materials to influence voter preference.

Consider the facts and circumstances that the IRS would deem relevant to determining whether the first example constitutes prohibited electioneering: Tax-exempt charities often wish to invite a well-known person to speak at their meetings or events because he or she is a public figure who will endorse and support the charity's tax-exempt mission.

But what if this person is also a candidate for election to a public office? The IRS has indicated that this may be accomplished without risking loss of tax-exempt status, but only if any activities that might act to influence an election are carefully excluded from the candidate's appearance at the event. Specifically, the candidate may only be invited to speak in his or her individual capacity — not as a candidate. Neither the candidate nor the tax-exempt organization may make any mention of the candidate's campaign or the election at the event, and no campaign activity or fundraising may take place in connection with the candidate's participation in the event. In the organization's communications announcing the candidate's attendance at the event, the organization should clearly state the capacity in which the candidate is appearing — as a victim of the illness the organization seeks to cure, for example, or as a long-time supporter of the organization's mission — and should not mention the individual's candidacy or the upcoming election.

If a candidate is invited to speak at a tax-exempt charity's event in a personal capacity and observes the restrictions noted above, it is not necessary for the organization to provide equal access to all other candidates for election to that office because the candidate's appearance will not involve the nonprofit charity in influencing an election.

But, in some cases, a tax-exempt charity may wish to invite an individual or individuals to speak at an organization event in their capacities as candidates. This, obviously, carries a greater risk of involving a nonprofit charity in prohibited electioneering. To avoid that, the IRS has advised that a charity must take steps at the event to ensure the following:

- It provides equal opportunity and access to all bona fide candidates who are seeking the same office.

- It does not represent that it supports or opposes any candidate (a statement to this effect should be made when the candidates are introduced and in the organization's communications concerning the candidates' attendance).

- It does not permit any election campaign fundraising at the event.

In determining whether candidates are being given an equal opportunity to participate, the organization should take into account the nature of the event to which each candidate is invited, as well as the manner of the presentation. A tax-exempt organization that invites one candidate to speak at its well-attended annual banquet, and invites the opposing candidate to speak at a local meeting that draws far fewer attendees, will likely be found by the IRS to have violated the electioneering prohibition, even if the manner of presentation for both speakers is otherwise neutral.

Are there any activities related to elections in which a charity can safely engage without incurring a violation? The following activities by a charitable organization should not subject it to charges of influencing an election — *provided* they are conducted in a scrupulously fair, nonpartisan, and unbiased way:

1. voter education

2. candidate debates or public forums

3. get-out-the-vote drives

Because the penalties for violation of the electioneering prohibition are so great, any public charity contemplating an activity that might be related in any way to an election should seek experienced legal counsel prior to undertaking the activity.

Personal Partisan Activity as an *Individual*

As we have seen, directors, officers, and employees of a charity are forbidden to engage in electioneering — but only in their roles as representatives or employees of the charity. Nothing in the law prohibits them as individuals from exercising their right to engage in partisan electioneering activities. Employees and directors can actively work for any candidate during after-work hours, while on leave without pay, or while using vacation leave.

But directors, officers, and employees must take care that their partisan activities are not perceived as being attributed to or associated with the charity. Officers and employees obviously should not make partisan comments in the organization's publications or at the charity's functions. But even if they speak or write on partisan electoral issues in forums not associated with the charity, they should — particularly during an election campaign — clearly state that their comments are personal and not intended to represent the views of the organization they work or volunteer for. If a director of a charity, in another example, allows his name to be listed in a campaign brochure as supporting a candidate, the director should ensure that he is not identified in the brochure as being associated in any way with the charity.

While the right of the individual citizen to engage in partisan election activity is paramount in our society, those governing or employed by a charity have a special duty to ensure that their personal political activities do not endanger the existence of the charitable organization they serve.

LOBBYING AND ELECTIONEERING BY NONCHARITABLE NONPROFITS

The federal tax law regarding nonprofit organizations that have qualified as tax-exempt other than as charitable organizations — e.g., social welfare organizations, unions, and trade associations — is considerably more flexible. Tax-exempt social welfare organizations (those organizations described in section 501(c)(4) of the Code) are permitted to conduct legislative activities without limit, so long as the lobbying advances their exempt purposes and does not deter the ability of the organizations to engage primarily in their tax-exempt activities. For this reason, charitable organizations sometimes create social welfare organizations as a tandem enterprise so that the social welfare organization can carry out the lobbying goals of the charitable organization under far fewer restrictions.

Similarly, a trade association that qualifies as tax exempt (those organizations described in section 501(c)(6) of the Code) is not limited in its lobbying activities as long as the lobbying advances its tax-exempt purposes and does not prevent it from primarily engaging in exempt activities. It should be noted, however, that lobbying activities of a trade association may result in adverse tax consequences for its members. In general, when a member pays dues to a trade association, those dues are tax deductible as a business expense; but, there is no business expense deduction for funds expended on lobbying. Therefore, when a trade association engages in lobbying, the portion of its members' dues allocable to the lobbying activities is not tax deductible for the member.

With regard to electioneering, social welfare organizations are generally not covered by the same restrictions on these activities that are applied to charitable organizations. Accordingly, a social welfare organization is permitted to engage in electioneering as long as this activity does not prevent it from undertaking its exempt functions. As for trade associations, federal tax law is silent on any limitation on electioneering by such organizations. As long as the activities are not so extensive that they interfere with the association carrying out its tax-exempt activities and purposes, electioneering is permitted for such an organization.

Electioneering by both social welfare organizations and trade associations is almost always carried on by PACs established by these organizations. Structuring campaign activities in this way keeps the parent organizations from becoming subject to a political organizations tax, which would otherwise apply if they engaged in election activities.

Social welfare organizations and trade associations can use their own money to fund the creation and operation of a PAC; federal election law refers to this as "soft money" expenditures. But contributions made to the campaigns of individual candidates for public office should come from PAC funds — so-called "hard money" — not from the funds of a parent public charity. Careful record keeping is necessary to ensure the proper use and characterization of these different types of funds, if the parent organization is to avoid adverse tax consequences.

Finally, there is a type of nonprofit organization that qualifies for tax-exempt status that undertakes political activities as its primary purpose. These organizations have grown rapidly and are now an important player in the political firmament in the United States. They are commonly referred to by the Code section under which they qualify for tax-exempt status: Section 527 organizations. Section 527 organizations, also known as political organizations, are organized and operated for the primary purpose of accepting contributions and making expenditures to influence the selection, nomination, election, or appointment of any individual to federal, state, or local public office or office in a political organization, or the election of presidential electors. They include political parties; federal, state, and local candidates committees; and political action committees. They have received a great deal of scrutiny in recent years, and now are required to periodically file public disclosure reports with the IRS, rather than the Federal Election Commission. This facilitates reporting of their contributions and disbursements so that their support and operations are publicly known in advance of elections.

CHAPTER Q&AS

Q: What is the difference between lobbying and electioneering?

A: Lobbying is an effort by an individual or organization to influence voting by members of a legislative body on legislation. The legislative body may be the U.S. Congress, a state legislature, or a local or municipal body with legislative powers. Electioneering, also known as political campaign activity, is the process of intervening (either for or against) in a campaign of a candidate for public office. Lobbying is generally permitted, to varying degrees, for nonprofit organizations that have federal tax-exempt status. Electioneering is prohibited for nonprofit charitable organizations under federal tax law, but is permissible under certain circumstances for other types of tax-exempt organizations.

Q: Can a candidate for public office who supports our mission speak at our charity's annual dinner without violating the rules against electioneering?

A: Yes, but only in his or her individual capacity — not as a candidate. Neither the candidate nor the charitable organization may make any mention of the candidate's campaign or the election at the event, and no campaign activity or fundraising may take place in connection with the candidate's participation in the event. In the organization's communication efforts to announce the candidate's attendance at the event, the organization should clearly state the capacity in which the candidate is appearing — as a victim of the illness that the organization seeks to cure, for example, or as a long-time supporter of the organization's mission — and it should not mention the individual's candidacy or the upcoming election.

Nonprofit boards of directors and their chief executives should fully understand the process of lobbying, its role in carrying out the mission of the organization, and the limits that apply to their organizations' ability to conduct lobbying activities. Lobbying is a constitutional right of nonprofit organizations and can be an extremely effective means of achieving the organization's goals. The chief executive must be familiar with the difference between direct and grass-roots lobbying and should work with counsel to determine the methodology for reporting lobbying activity that will provide the greatest amount of flexibility. The board and the chief executive should also work with counsel to examine other structural options that may permit the organization to conduct greater amounts of lobbying should it become necessary. Just as important, the board and the chief executive should understand the difference between lobbying and electioneering. They must understand the impact of different types of tax-exempt status on the ability of the organization to be involved in political campaign activity, and be clear on the absolute prohibition against electioneering by charitable organizations.

QUESTIONS THE BOARD SHOULD ASK

- Is every board member actively engaged in advocating for our mission?

- If we regularly engage in lobbying, have we considered making the 501(h) election?

- Does our Form 990 correctly reflect our lobbying activities?

5.
Intellectual Property: Trademarks and Copyrights

E. Scott Johnson

Intellectual property — products of human intellect that are accorded propertylike legal status — are "hidden" assets of many nonprofits of which directors and managers may be unaware. Yet, such property has taken on increased value in today's world: The distinctive logo that identifies a national nonprofit of impeccable reputation; the award-winning newsletter published by a nonprofit; the artistic creations that result from a playwrights' workshop run by a nonprofit theater; the therapy for rheumatoid arthritis developed at a nonprofit research hospital — all are extremely valuable assets to those nonprofits. Board members and senior staff need to recognize the importance of these assets and guide their nonprofit toward the best policies and practices to enhance and protect the value of those assets, avoid their forfeiture, and eliminate the risk of violating or infringing the property of others.

Intellectual property has long referred to copyrightable works of authorship, inventions, trademarks, and trade secrets. But the term is more expansively used today to include such things as licensable know-how, domain names, biological materials, and the list continues to grow.

Nonprofits routinely create, use, publish, and sell works embodying intellectual property. The name of the organization and its branded products, services, and publications are its trademarks. The photographs, graphics, images, textual works, and artwork it publishes or makes accessible on its Web site are its copyrightable works. All are valuable assets that need to be recognized and protected by nonprofit organizations.

WHAT ARE THE BASIC CONCEPTS?

When intellectual property is created by employees, volunteers, or vendors of a nonprofit, the organization should usually ensure that it acquires the rights to that property. For example, if the organization engages a consultant to write a manual or series of articles, the organization will probably want to acquire the exclusive right to publish those works. Yet without a written agreement that specifically assigns the copyright to the organization, the consultant by law retains the copyright and gives to the organization only a license to use his work. Under the U.S. Copyright Act, when no written agreement addresses copyright ownership, those rights are given to the author of a commissioned work. The author is also free to adapt or publish that work on his own, or to license it to others.

When a nonprofit wishes to use intellectual property belonging to others, it must go through rights clearance, the process of securing rights, permissions, or licenses to use others' intellectual property. Rights clearance may be required for uses of text, artwork, sound recordings, audiovisual works, trademarks, and photographs. For example, to use a photograph in a print advertisement, one must first secure a license from the owner of the photograph copyright — usually the photographer, a stock photo house, or a publisher. To use a photograph containing an identifiable living person in advertising, one must also secure a release from that person — or risk liability for infringing his or her right of privacy or publicity.

There is a common misconception that nonprofits, particularly tax-exempt charitable organizations, are entitled to a "fair use" exemption for using others' intellectual property. While there are a few specific exemptions for nonprofits in copyright law, nonprofits generally must adhere to the same rules as for-profit organizations when using copyrighted works. At the same time, nonprofits are entitled to enjoy all of the benefits and protections of intellectual property laws that for-profits do. If a nonprofit owns valuable intellectual property, it can expect for that property the same safeguards and rewards as a for-profit corporation does for its material.

TRADEMARKS

Product names, logos, and slogans can become valuable assets to a nonprofit organization, attracting purchasers, contributors, and members who respect and rely on the quality of branded programs, services, and products. Nonprofits have established valuable goodwill in such well-known names as UNITED WAY®, MAKE A WISH®, and CONSUMER REPORTS®.

Trademarks usually have little or no value initially, but can dramatically appreciate in value through successful, widespread, and continuing use by a nonprofit. Unlike copyrights and patents that eventually expire, trademark rights can be renewed indefinitely — as long as the trademark remains in use. Because a trademark is an appreciating asset with a potentially perpetual life, it is important to choose trademarks carefully and to protect them through federal registration and controlled licensing.

WHAT IS A TRADEMARK?

A *trademark* is any word, symbol, design, or a combination of words and design (each a "mark") that identifies and distinguishes one person's or entity's goods or services from those of another. For example, the words GIRL SCOUT COOKIES® and EXCEDRIN® are both trademarks, as are the Ralston Purina Checkerboard Square design and the hourglass-shaped COCA-COLA® bottle configuration. A slogan (e.g., A MIND IS A TERRIBLE THING TO WASTE®) can also be a trademark.

If words and design elements (such as a logo) are used together, the combination can be registered as a *composite* mark. However, separate registration of design and word elements is also often useful for this reason: When determining whether a trademark has been infringed, the law requires trademarks to be evaluated as a whole and not dissected. When determining whether a trademark that combines a logo with words has been infringed, the words would be considered integral to the logo design. Therefore, if an alleged infringement involved only the logo and not the words, the trademark owner's case for infringement could be substantially weakened by the inclusion of words in its trademark registration.

When used to identify a service, the mark is called a *service mark*. For example, REACH OUT AND TOUCH SOMEONE® is a service mark for long-distance telephone services. Marks can function as both trademarks and service marks (e.g., LEXUS® is both a trademark for automobiles and a service mark when used to advertise automobile repair services). Because trademark law is based on the idea that trademarks serve as badges of quality, legal protections exist to guard the public from deception and confusion, as well as the trademark owner's goodwill in the mark.

Trademarks today also include Internet domain names, and some domain names have become valuable intellectual property. Domain names may be registered as trademarks or service marks if they meet the statutory criteria and function to distinguish the products or services of one entity from another. However, unlike the general marketplace in which many companies sometimes use the same name on unrelated products, each domain name is unique. If five different nonprofits offer a product or service under the name "ABC," each in a different field, only the first to register the "abc.org" domain name will be entitled to use it.

REGISTERING AND PROTECTING A TRADEMARK

Trademark rights can be established simply by being the first to use a mark in commerce. Regardless of whether the mark is registered, the law generally affords the first to use a mark (the "senior user") legal protection against infringement within its trading area. Trademark rights are infringed when a "junior user" uses a confusingly similar mark for the same or related goods or services, creating a *likelihood of confusion*, which is the legal test for trademark infringement. An additional cause of action for dilution of trademark rights is available for *famous* marks, even when the mark is used for unrelated goods or services.

A trademark does not achieve the greatest legal protection in the United States until it is federally registered. It is possible and advisable to reserve rights in a mark prior to its use by filing an intent-to-use application with the U.S. Patent & Trademark Office (PTO). Even though certain legal rights (common-law rights) can be claimed based solely on the prior use of a mark, federal registration provides additional important advantages, including

1. access to federal courts;

2. the ability to recover profits, damages, and costs in an infringement action (including the possibility of treble damages and attorneys' fees);

3. constructive notice of ownership of the trademark, eliminating a good faith defense by anyone adopting the mark subsequent to the registrant's date of registration;

4. evidence of the validity of the registration and the facts asserted in the registration;

5. possible "incontestability" status after five years.

To protect its intellectual property, a nonprofit should secure the services of an attorney experienced in trademark law. The first step the attorney will take in order to obtain federal registration will be to undertake a trademark search to determine whether any other person or entity can claim prior rights in the mark. An online search of PTO records will be conducted first, followed by a full trademark search.

(Logo designs require different searching strategies, and it is impossible to search designs as thoroughly as words. Typically, the design search is confined to a review of similar designs in the PTO records.) The trademark search should reveal whether another user or registrant of the same or a similar mark has established rights in the relevant field of goods or services.

Trademark search reports provide raw data that must be interpreted and evaluated by a professional. For example, a potentially conflicting mark may not be identical (marks need not be identical to infringe), may be used for different goods or services, or a pattern of litigation may show up in the PTO file history — all of which need to be evaluated by counsel to determine whether a proposed use poses real risks.

Once it is determined that a trademark is available, actual use should commence as soon as possible; or, if use cannot be immediately initiated, an intent-to-use application should be filed. But use is ultimately required to secure federal registration, and enforceable rights do not mature until actual use of the mark has begun. It must be a bona fide use of the mark, in interstate commerce, in the ordinary course of trade. For purposes of establishing a date of first use and qualifying for registration of a trademark, the trademarked goods must be shipped to an independent recipient in another state. For service marks, the qualifying use is an advertising use in interstate commerce, such as advertising in a publication or a direct mailing that crosses state lines.

Once the nonprofit's application for registration is made, the PTO examination process normally takes about one year, depending upon the nature and extent of any objections raised by the PTO's examining attorney. Marks that pass muster under the Trademark Act are registered on the PTO's Principal Register.

In contrast, *descriptive* marks are initially registered on the PTO's Supplemental Register. While descriptive marks can be registered, generic terms like "apple" for the fruit, as opposed to "APPLE" for computers, which is not generic. Generic terms cannot be protected as trademarks because one may not claim exclusive rights in generic words that are used in the name of a product or service.

While descriptive marks are afforded some initial rights under the federal Trademark Act, including the right to use the ® symbol and to bring an infringement action in federal court, registration on the Supplemental Register does not provide the full scope of legal benefits accorded to marks registered on the Principal Register.

Descriptive marks (e.g., AFTER TAN® for tanning lotion; FOOD FAIR® for grocery store services) are not eligible for full trademark protection initially, but may become so after acquiring *secondary meaning*. Secondary meaning (as opposed to primary "descriptive" meaning) arises for a mark that, although descriptive, has also become associated in a purchaser's mind with a specific source or sponsorship of the goods or services, usually established through long use and advertising. A descriptive trademark in continuous use without adverse adjudication of rights for five years is presumed under the law to have acquired a secondary meaning, and then application may be made to move it to the Principal Register.

Unlike copyrights and patents, which are accorded a limited duration of protection, trademark rights can last indefinitely if the mark continues to be in use. The term of a federal trademark registration is 10 years, indefinitely renewable for 10-year terms.

It is a good practice to use the symbol ™ in superscript immediately adjacent to all uses of unregistered marks. This symbol provides notice of the user's claim of proprietary rights. The ™ symbol is also commonly used by an applicant while awaiting approval of the federal application. Once the federal registration is obtained, the trademark should be displayed with the ® symbol. (Premature use of the ® symbol can impair the federal registration or the maintenance of an infringement action.)

A nonprofit can license its trademark to a third party, but care must be taken in drafting license agreements; otherwise, trademark rights can be impaired. A trademark license must contain provisions controlling uses of the licensed marks and the quality of goods or services sold under marks. Trademark rights can be lost through uncontrolled licensing if the mark ceases to serve as a badge of quality for goods or services.

Trademarks are generally issued by each nation and separate registrations must be made to obtain a trademark in a foreign country. A nonprofit should evaluate its U.S. trademark to determine whether the marks should be protected from infringement in other countries. Already possessing a U.S. trademark registration may aid in securing trademark rights in other countries.

COPYRIGHT

Copyright law extends legal protection to the authors and owners of "original works of authorship" in six broadly construed categories: literary works; musical works; choreographic works; pictorial, graphic, and sculptural works; motion pictures and other audiovisual works; and sound recordings. (Literary works include computer programs, because computer programming source code consists of characters and symbols.) Copyright does not protect all written works. For example, titles, names, short phrases, or slogans, are not protectable under copyright law (but may be protectable as trademarks, depending upon the usage).

While textual works are copyrightable, the information expressed in factual works, such as historical facts or scientific data, is not. Ideas, procedures, methods, systems, processes, and discoveries are not protected by copyright (although they may be protectable as trade secrets or by patent if the legal tests for patentability are met). Copyright can protect compilations of data (including automated databases), even if the underlying data are in the public domain.

The owner of a copyright has an exclusive right to

- reproduce the copyrighted work in copies;

- prepare derivative works or adaptations based upon the copyrighted work;

- distribute copies of the work by sale or transfer of ownership, or by rental, lease, or lending;

- perform the work publicly in the case of most categories or work; and

- display the copyrighted work publicly.

These are *economic* rights, and do not always include *authorization* rights. For example, in the United States, once a song has been released on records, tapes, or CDs, another recording artist may release his or her version of that song without first securing authorization from the copyright owner, under the compulsory licensing provisions of the U.S. Copyright Act. The song's copyright owner may not prohibit another artist from re-recording and distributing his or her version of the song, so long as the licensing payment required by the statute is made, thereby satisfying the copyright owner's economic rights under the Copyright Act.

In most instances, the owner of the copyright is its actual author. For example, the person who writes an article or computer program source code usually owns the copyright. That is not the case when an employee creates a copyrightable work within the scope of his or her employment. If an employee writes an article for use on a nonprofit organization's Web site or computer code to streamline the organization's grants-application process, the organization automatically owns the text of the article and the computer code as works-made-for-hire and the nonprofit, not the employee, is considered the author of those works under U.S. copyright law.

If a copyrightable work is created by an employee of a nonprofit, but the work is not within the scope of employment, then the employee retains the copyright. For example, an employee writes grant applications for a nonprofit during the work day and writes poetry in the evening and on weekends. That employee owns the copyright in the poetry, but the nonprofit owns the copyright in the grant applications written by the employee as a work-made-for-hire. Sometimes what is "within the scope of employment" is less clear, as when a nonprofit's bookkeeper develops accounting software at home on his or her own time. But in most cases, a review of the employee's job description or duties will make it fairly obvious whether a particular work is a work-made-for-hire. Nevertheless, if there is any question about whether a work by an employee will technically be considered a work for hire, the nonprofit should acquire copyright ownership by written assignment from the employee.

Attention to the legal requirements for acquisition of copyright is especially important when a work is commissioned by a nonprofit from an independent contractor. While a common sense understanding of the words "work-made-for-hire" could lead one to conclude that the copyright in a commissioned work would belong to the party paying for the work, this often is not the case. Except for nine specific categories of works (a contribution to a collective work; part of an audiovisual work; a translation; a supplementary work; a compilation; an instructional text; a test; answer material for a test; or an atlas), works prepared by independent contractors are *not* works-made-for-hire, and copyright ownership must be acquired by written assignment from the independent contractor.

For most commissioned works, the magic words assigning the copyright to the nonprofit must appear in a written contract between the parties. The adverse consequences for a nonprofit neglecting to do so are illustrated by this example: If a nonprofit theater sponsors a play-writing workshop and invites playwrights to participate, unless the theater signs a contract with each participant providing that the theater owns the copyright to any works resulting from workshop, the playwrights will own the copyrights and may license the copyrighted works to other theaters or producers — including competitors of the nonprofit theater that paid for the development of the artistic works.

For works created on or after January 1, 1978, the term of copyright dates from its creation and endures for a term consisting of the life of the author plus 70 years after the author's death. In the case of joint works, copyright endures for a term consisting of the life of the last surviving author plus 70 years after the last surviving author's death. In the case of works-made-for-hire, copyright endures for a term of 95 years from the year of its first publication, or a term of 120 years from the year of its creation, whichever expires first. (Works published before January 1, 1978, may remain in copyright or may be in the public domain, depending upon the year of first publication, whether a required renewal application was filed, and the nationality of the authors.)

COPYRIGHT REGISTRATION AND PROTECTION

Original works of authorship are registered through application to the U.S. Copyright Office. Copyright registration secures important rights. Unlike trademarks, copyright registration is a prerequisite for bringing a copyright infringement claim, and registration prior to infringement preserves important remedies, including the availability of statutory damages (up to $150,000 per infringed work, even in the absence of any damages or infringer's profits) and attorneys' fees. When registration is secured within five years after first publication of the work, the registration constitutes *prima facie* evidence of the validity of the copyright and the facts stated in the Registration Certificate.

Registration of copyright is invaluable for an early and simple resolution of infringement claims, and may provide the means for enhancing damages awards. Another benefit of copyright registration is recordation of title in the searchable databases of the U.S. Copyright Office, which can be important in various transactions, including those where recording security interests, assignments, or exclusive licenses are important, and reference to specific copyright registrations is required or desirable. Copyright registrants also have the right to prohibit the importation of infringing works by recording the registration with the U.S. Customs Service.

Providing notice to the public of a copyright was for many years a tricky issue for copyright owners. The failure to include a copyright notice in a work (or, in some cases, if the notice was defective) divested the copyright owner of its copyright. Many valuable copyrights fell into the public domain for that reason. But since 1989, when the United States joined the Berne Convention for the Protection of Literary and Artistic Works (referred to as the "Berne Convention") on copyrights, the omission of copyright notice in published works no longer automatically strips the owner of a copyright. However, it is still advisable to use a copyright notice, both to deter infringers and to eliminate the "innocent infringer" defense, which can be asserted under certain conditions, such as absence of copyright notice. A proper copyright notice is in this format:

Copyright© **[Year]** by **[Copyright Owner]**

The Copyright Act protects copyrighted works by providing that the unauthorized use of a copyrighted work by copying, distributing, transmitting, performing, displaying, or creating a new work that adapts a copyrighted work, infringes the copyright owner's exclusive rights. A work need not be identical to infringe. The legal test is substantial similarity as determined by the ordinary observer. *Substantial similarity* can be based on quantitative, qualitative, or general look-and-feel comparisons of the copyrighted work with the infringing work.

Obtaining a U.S. copyright generally does not provide protection abroad. If a U.S. copyright is infringed in a foreign country, the copyright owner usually cannot bring an infringement case in a U.S. court nor seek remedies under U.S. copyright law in a foreign court. In most instances, the copyright owner will need to bring its copyright infringement claim in a court in the foreign country where the infringement occurred, but under that country's laws.

Some unlicensed uses are defensible as "fair use" under a four-factor test set forth in the U.S. Copyright Act. In addition, there are a few specific exemptions from copyright protection that provide a right to utilize a copyrighted work in a particular manner. It is important to remember, however, that fair use is a *defense* to a copyright infringement claim, *not* an affirmative right. For that reason, many organizations routinely seek permissions or licenses even when the contemplated use would likely be a fair use.

Copyright litigation can be very expensive, and nonprofits, of course, are not immune from copyright infringement lawsuits. So a nonprofit organization that regularly publishes newsletters, books, or audiovisual works should obtain media perils "errors & omissions" insurance to protect itself from the costs of infringement liability.

Although there is no international copyright protection, the Berne Convention is the oldest international copyright agreement. Its member countries agree to accord minimum standards of protection to citizens of other signatory countries and to protect their works even if the formalities of registration are not followed in their country. Because the United States has joined the Berne Convention, U.S. copyright holders have minimum protections in a number of other foreign countries.

In addition, the United States has copyright treaties directly with many nations that provide full and automatic protection for U.S. copyright owners under the copyright laws of those countries. But treaties that provide reciprocal protection mean only that protection of a copyrighted U.S. work in a foreign country is limited to that provided by the foreign copyright law — which may or may not be equivalent to U.S. copyright law. Nevertheless, the copyrights of U.S. citizens have at least some level of protection in virtually every country in the world, either by treaty or international convention.

PATENTS

Patent law, like copyright law, is mandated in the U.S. Constitution, which directs Congress to enact laws that will provide incentives to inventors by protecting their works. A *patent* is a grant from the government, giving the patent owner the right to exclude others from making, using, or selling the patented invention in the United States. In order to secure patent protection, the claimed invention must consist of unique and useful subject matter, which generally falls into one of three categories:

1. utility patents, such as a machine, composition of matter, or process;

2. plant patents (asexually reproduced plants); and

3. design patents, for the ornamental design of a utilitarian object.

Nonprofit organizations are rarely in the position of manufacturing consumer products that need patent protection. For this reason, a thorough discussion of patents is not included here. But the reader should note that, in 1998, the Supreme Court expanded the scope of patent law to include new business methods, precipitating a flood of business method patent filings, particularly related to the Internet and e-commerce. Business method patents are controversial in both the legal and business communities, and have attracted media attention, such as Amazon.com's lawsuit against Barnes & Noble for allegedly infringing its "1-Click" online ordering method patent, and the electrical engineer who won a $35 million award against e-Bay for infringing his online auction method patent. With the advent of business method patents, patent infringement exposure is greater because business method patents are being obtained for a wide range of business practices. Companies engaged in e-commerce, especially in the health care and the financial services fields, have been very proactive in obtaining business method patents, and in some cases extracting license fees from those utilizing online business models that allegedly infringe.

While nonprofits may be less likely to own or develop property that qualifies for patent protection, they are still vulnerable to claims of patent infringement. For example, if a nonprofit utilizes a novel business method in its online operations, and a patent on the business method later is issued to someone else, the patent holder may send the nonprofit a cease-and-desist letter or demand that the nonprofit pay for a license to continue using the business method. Even though the organization adopted the business method without receiving any prior notice of the pending patent, the nonprofit may still be liable for patent infringement. (If it was a copyright infringement claim, the nonprofit could assert independent creation as a complete defense, but independent creation is not a defense to a patent-infringement claim.)

If a nonprofit organization receives a cease-and-desist letter based on patent infringement, it is important to contact legal counsel promptly. When an opinion of counsel is obtained and followed, the organization relying on the opinion may avoid the greater damages possible in cases of willful infringement.

Chapter Q&As

Q: Aren't nonprofit organizations exempt from the copyright, trademark, and patent laws?

A: There is a common misconception that nonprofits, particularly tax-exempt charitable organizations, are entitled to a "fair use" exemption for using others' intellectual property. While there are a few specific exemptions for nonprofits in copyright law, nonprofits generally must adhere to the same rules as for-profit organizations when using copyrighted works. At the same time, nonprofits are entitled to enjoy all of the benefits and protections of intellectual property laws that for-profits do. If a nonprofit owns valuable intellectual property, it can expect for that property the same safeguards and rewards to which a for-profit corporation is entitled.

Q: Who has the right to use materials created by our nonprofit organization's employees, volunteers, and independent contractors?

A: When intellectual property is created by employees, volunteers, or independent contractors of a nonprofit, the organization should usually ensure that it acquires the rights to that property. In most instances, the owner of the copyright is its actual author. That is not the case when an employee creates a copyrightable work within the scope of his or her employment. For example, if an employee writes an article for use on a nonprofit organization's Web site or computer code to streamline the organization's grants-application process, the organization automatically owns the text of the article and the computer code as works-made-for-hire and the nonprofit, not the employee, is considered the "author" of those works under U.S. copyright law. If a copyrightable work is created by an employee of a nonprofit, but the work is not within the scope of employment, then the employee retains the copyright. Attention to the legal requirements for acquisition of copyright is especially important when a work is commissioned by a nonprofit from an independent contractor. Except for certain categories of works, materials prepared by independent contractors are *not* works-made-for-hire, and copyright ownership must be acquired by written assignment from the independent contractor.

The intellectual property of a nonprofit organization is often one of its greatest assets, and the chief executive and the board of directors must take great care to protect the organization's rights in that asset. Directors must appreciate the value of intellectual property assets and guide the organization in adopting best practices and policies that will enhance them, protect against their forfeiture, and likewise ensure that the organization does not infringe upon the intellectual property rights of others. The chief executive should work with counsel to ensure that copyright protection has been obtained for the images, graphics, artwork, written works, and similar materials of the organization where appropriate. Similarly, trademark protection should be considered for the name and logo of the organization, particularly where similar names and logos may be used by other organizations. The board and the chief executive should consider opportunities to share rights to intellectual property with employees of the organization as an incentive to promote greater creativity.

- Is our organization well protected against forfeiture of our intellectual property? Have we identified all the areas to be protected?

- Do we have a process to protect our own intellectual capital when we collaborate with other organizations and individuals?

6.
Employment Law

Pamela J. White

All private employers — including nonprofit organizations — are bound by an increasing number of statutory and case-law mandates affecting the employer-employee relationship. Historically, that relationship has been considered "at will," meaning the employee can quit at any time and the employer can likewise exercise its discretion to terminate the relationship at any time. The at-will employment relationship can be terminated by either party for any reason or for no reason at all.

But the "at-will" employment tradition has been increasingly eroded by federal and state statutes that regulate employer practices. These restrictions must prompt greater attention to human resource policies by nonprofit employers. Nonprofit organizations today must adhere to basic statutory protections of employees, such as wage payment laws; to nondiscrimination in hiring and in the workplace; to consistency in the application of personnel policies; and to basic fairness in disciplinary practices. Nonprofit organizations are also not immune from violent incidents in the workplace, which raise workplace safety and employee security issues. Twenty-first century technologies in the workplace raise questions about protecting proprietary information, employers' monitoring practices, and employee privacy protections.

As a part of its role in overseeing the operations of the organization, and in order to adequately discharge its fiduciary duty of care, the board of directors of a nonprofit organization should have the opportunity to review the human resources policies developed by the organization's staff. While it may not be necessary for the board to review the content of every policy, the board should be satisfied that the organization is in compliance with current employment law standards for such policies. In addition to working with staff in this regard, the board could also confer with counsel or an outside consultant as to the adequacy of its policies. There are exceptions, however, to this general rule of thumb. For example, if the board or chief executive becomes aware that there have been abuses in a particular area, such as repeated incidents of sexual harassment, or multiple financial irregularities, the board should become more directly involved and should ensure that these problems have been addressed with appropriate remedial policies. Also, the board may wish to have a more hands-on role with respect to the development of policies in areas where the board wants the organization to be more proactive, such as the promotion of diversity within the organization and its programs. Another exception would be in those instances where regulators, such as a state attorney general or an insurance commissioner, are investigating or challenging the actions of the organization. In such cases, the board may have to be more directly involved in the development and approval of HR policies than would normally be necessary.

As employees' statutory rights have expanded, claims of wrongful discharge have increased. And as the number and magnitude of employment-related claims has escalated, so has the potential financial risk to nonprofit employers. In addition to the cost of any judgments, just defending such claims can be costly, even when the organization is not at fault or the claim is groundless or fraudulent. However, alternative dispute resolution procedures are expanding, and courts are encouraging mandatory arbitration of statutory and contract claims.

Most states and state courts still adhere to the employment-at-will rule (in the absence of a written agreement between employer and employee that specifies a term of employment or provides for dismissal in specified causes). However, application of the at-will rule has been eroded by developments in two areas: enactment of specific laws and regulations restricting the at-will tradition, and common-law developments in case law affecting the employment relationship.

LAWS AND REGULATIONS THAT AFFECT EMPLOYMENT RELATIONSHIPS

FAIR LABOR STANDARDS ACT (FLSA)

The FLSA is the comprehensive federal law governing employee wages, permitted hours of work, and basic employee record keeping. Regulations governing minimum wages and overtime are comprehensive and voluminous, although frequently ignored by employers even in the face of severe penalties for noncompliance. The FLSA regulations can be complicated and employers seeking simplicity often declare workers to be exempt from the requirements of overtime compensation — without actually satisfying the standards for determining the professional, administrative, or executive status of employees that might exempt employees from overtime compensation.

Under the Fair Labor Standards Act, "nonexempt" employees (that is, those who are not exempt from the FLSA overtime requirements) must be compensated at or above the minimum wage for all hours worked. The FLSA requires employers to pay overtime to nonexempt employees at a rate of one and one-half times their regular rate of pay for each hour worked over 40 in a work week. The regular rate of pay includes all remuneration for employment paid to the employee, except certain excluded forms of compensation, such as payments of gifts or discretionary bonuses and payments made when no work was performed.

The FLSA and state law equivalents also establish record-keeping requirements for all employers, including nonprofits. The records that must be kept include hours worked each workday and total hours worked each workweek; total daily or weekly straight-time earnings or wages due for hours worked (exclusive of overtime); total wages paid each pay period; and total additions to or deductions from wages paid each pay period. The U.S. Department of Labor and similar state agencies may conduct FLSA investigations, which can include a review of an employer's records. Violations of the record-keeping requirements or any of the other FLSA provisions can result in civil monetary penalties. Other violations may also result in back-pay awards, plus liquidated damages awards and attorney's fees.

Of all of the employment laws, nonprofit organizations typically encounter the most compliance problems in the area of payment of wages. Experience has shown that nonprofit organizations often run afoul of the overtime and minimum wage provisions. They also, however unwittingly, may improperly use volunteers in violation of these rules. Accordingly, board members and the chief executive should pay particular attention to ensuring that the organization's policies and procedures are compliant and up to date in this area.

STATE WAGES AND WORK HOURS LAWS

Wage payment statutes in each state provide that employers must establish regular pay periods, generally biweekly or semimonthly; establish and inform employees of basic salary or hourly wage rates; provide gross-earning statements and identify authorized deductions for each pay period; and provide advance notice of any changes. Wages generally are defined as all compensation due to employees for work performed, including salary, nondiscretionary bonuses, commissions, fringe benefits, and any other remuneration promised for service. Employers may not withhold earned compensation or make deductions from paychecks due, including final paychecks, without express written approval by employees. Whether an employer must pay a departing employee the value of vacation time accrued but unused depends on if the employer has promised to do so by policy or in practice over time.

TAX LAW

Federal and state tax laws require nonprofit employers to pay a payroll tax on their employees' wages and to withhold income taxes from their paychecks. This is *not* the case for independent contractors. Sometimes employers will seek to avoid having to pay employee benefits and payroll taxes and to withhold taxes by mischaracterizing an employee as a contract worker or independent contractor. Whether the IRS will agree with such characterization, or instead determine the worker is an employee, depends primarily on the amount of control exercised by the nonprofit over the work performed. The more direction and control wielded by the organization as to hours worked, tasks assigned, location and supervision of performance, tools and work support available, the more likely that an employment relationship exists.

The totality of circumstances and economic realities should be carefully examined when making the employee versus contractor determination. This includes evaluating the nature and degree of the employer's control as to the manner in which the work is to be performed; whether the person's opportunity for profit or loss is dependent on his own skills; the extent of the person's investment in equipment, materials, and his own workers' equipment; the requirement of specialized skills; the duration of the working relationship; and the extent to which the service performed constitutes an integral part of the organization's own business. The IRS takes a dim view of mischaracterizing employees as independent contractors and nonprofits should take these determinations seriously.

BENEFITS OF WORKERS' COMPENSATION

State workers' compensation statutes provide employees injured on the job with certain financial and medical benefits. Statutes generally protect employees injured by accidents arising out of and in the course of employment, as well as for occupational diseases. [Employers also may be responsible to accommodate employees according to the Family and Medical Leave Act (FMLA) and the Americans with Disabilities Act (ADA).] Workers' compensation laws also commonly prohibit termination for having filed a workers' compensation claim.

Finally, restrictions on the employer-employee relationship may appear incidentally in a number of other statutes. For example, federal Occupational Safety & Health Act (OSHA) regulations prohibit termination of an employee for reporting an OSHA violation by an employer.

DISCRIMINATION IN THE WORKPLACE

Title VII of the Civil Rights Act of 1964 (Title VII)

This federal statute prohibits discrimination on the basis of race, color, religion, sex, or national origin in hiring, discharge, compensation, and any terms, conditions, or privileges of employment. Title VII also bars retaliation against employees for making discrimination complaints. Covered employers include nonprofit organizations that have 15 or more employees for each working day in each of 20 or more calendar weeks in the current or preceding year.

Employees pursuing charges with the Equal Employment Opportunity Commission (EEOC) and lawsuits to enforce Title VII rights must present evidence that the employer's variable or disparate treatment of employees implies a discriminatory motivation on the employer's part. The employer, in turn, can defend by identifying legitimate, nondiscriminatory reasons for its decisions. An employee who prevails against an employer may be entitled to reinstatement; front pay; back pay; attorney's fees; an injunction against the prohibited discrimination; compensatory damages for pain and suffering, financial loss, and mental anguish; and punitive damages. Compensatory and punitive damages are capped at certain amounts based on the size of the employer's work force, although the caps do not limit the amount of back pay or interest on back pay, front pay, or attorney's fees awarded to a prevailing plaintiff in jury trials.

Claims of sexual harassment and pregnancy discrimination are covered under Title VII's prohibition of discrimination on the basis of sex. Sexual and other types of harassment are actionable when employees are subject to unwelcome verbal or physical conduct of a sexual, racial, or religious nature, or which conduct is made a condition of employment, such as a *quid pro quo* demand for sexual favors. Harassment also is actionable when the offensive conduct is intended or effectively is of such a nature as to unreasonably interfere with the employee's job performance or otherwise creates a hostile or abusive work environment. An employer will be automatically liable for a supervisor's harassment if that conduct results in a tangible employment action. Examples of tangible employment actions include hiring and firing; promotion and failure to promote; demotion; undesirable reassignment; a decision causing a significant change in benefits; a compensation decision; and work assignments.

Employers have the affirmative obligation at all times to maintain a workplace free of harassment and to address any claims of sexual harassment that arise. Trying to determine if employee misconduct constitutes sexual harassment can be difficult task. But any successful defense to a sexual harassment claim hinges in great part on a nonprofit having a valid and comprehensive sexual harassment prevention program. In order to avoid liability for employee claims of sexual harassment, employers must be able to show that they acted reasonably and promptly to investigate any employee complaints of harassment and to discipline or discharge employees found to be guilty of violating that policy. Failure to discharge or discipline employees for offending conduct will likely result in liability. In addition, employers should establish penalties for supervisors who fail to report complaints of sexual harassment or who fail to take immediate corrective action to respond to such complaints.

Instances also exist where employee religious beliefs may require reasonable accommodation of religious tenets by the employer. Employees must be afforded opportunity for religious observances and bona fide religious practice. There are additional circumstances where an employer's bona fide religious purposes permit that employer to institute religious requirements in hiring.

Title VII and other discrimination and wage statutes expressly prohibit retaliation against an employee or applicant for complaining of discrimination, or for participating in investigatory or agency proceedings, or for good faith opposition to unlawful practices. An employee claiming retaliation need not defend the merits of the underlying claim, but only show that the consequence of complaining or opposing bad practices was termination or other detrimental job action. Employers should amply document their personnel actions and business decisions that affect employees so as to demonstrate the absence of retaliation.

Americans with Disabilities Act (ADA)

The federal ADA prohibits employment discrimination against a *qualified individual* when the discrimination is based on that individual's disability. The ADA defines a qualified individual as someone "with a disability who, with or without reasonable accommodation, can perform the essential functions of the employment position that such individual holds or desires."

A disabled individual under the ADA is one who has a major life impairment, such as blindness, paralysis, deafness, or the like. The ADA requires an employer to make reasonable accommodation to permit a disabled but qualified employee to perform the essential functions of his or her job, to be fair in testing applicants, and to permit a disabled individual to enjoy benefits and privileges of employment that are equal to, or substantially equal to, those benefits and privileges afforded to similarly situated, nondisabled individuals. Reasonable accommodation may include making existing facilities accessible, restructuring jobs, modifying work schedules, reassigning employees, or making any other workplace modifications that the employer can accomplish without undue hardship. An undue hardship is considered an action that would require significant difficulty or expense to the employer when considered in light of such factors as the nature and cost of the accommodation needed, the overall financial resources of the facility or employer involved, and the employer's type of operation.

The ADA prohibits an employer from asking in a job interview about the existence, nature, or severity of a disability. The person interviewing for the organization may ask about an applicant's ability to perform specific job-related functions, but may not ask about disabilities. Once the job offer has been made, however, the employer may ask about the nature and extent of a disability, so long as the questions pertain to the essential job functions and are asked of all employees in that job category. If a job offer is withdrawn after the interview process, it can be withdrawn only for job-related reasons consistent with business necessity, and the organization should be prepared to demonstrate that the employee cannot perform the essential job functions, even with reasonable accommodation.

In addition, an employer may not require an applicant to submit to a pre-employment physical, but may require a physical once a job offer has been made. Any medical information obtained from the physical must be maintained in a file separate from the employee's general personnel file and must remain confidential.

Special problems may be posed by employees protected under the ADA who are recovering from substance abuse and participating in rehabilitation programs. For example, a hospital employee in a rehabilitation program is protected under the ADA, but drug and alcohol testing may nevertheless be required and justified to ensure the safety of those hospital patients whom the employee is treating or working with during his or her rehabilitation. Safety considerations are paramount in the discipline of employees posing a threat in the workplace by intoxication or other impairment. Effective drug and alcohol testing protocols require attention by managers, working closely with legal counsel.

Age Discrimination in Employment Act (ADEA)

The federal ADEA protects employees over the age of 40 from discrimination on the basis of age with regard to hiring, discharge, compensation, and other terms, conditions, or privileges of employment. Further, employers are prohibited from retaliating against an employee for asserting his or her rights under the ADEA and from publishing any notice or job advertisement that expresses any age preference or limitation.

An employee proving a claim of age discrimination may be entitled to back pay and fringe benefits, including interest, attorney's fees and costs, and reinstatement or front pay. In addition, if the employee can prove that the employer committed a "willful violation" of the ADEA, he or she may recover additional damages in an amount equal to the award for back pay and benefits. (These are not considered to be punitive damages.) Lawsuits under the ADEA are not subject to the compensatory and punitive damage caps that apply to Title VII and ADA claims. Amendments to the ADEA by the federal Older Worker Benefit Protection Act (OWBPA) specify for employers the proper procedures and disclosures to be made when older workers are involved in a company "downsizing" and are offered severance packages for releases and waivers of discrimination claims.

Section 1981 of the Reconstruction Era Civil Rights Act of 1866 (Section 1981)

This 19th-century law prohibits racial or national origin discrimination in the making and enforcement of contracts, which may include any form of employment relationship. Section 1981 claims may address all forms of intentional racial bias in the workplace in hiring, firing, disciplining, promoting, and compensating employees, and in working conditions. Procedural instructions in the Civil Rights Act of 1991 made clear that plaintiffs may request a jury trial and recover both compensatory and punitive damages from defendants acting with callous indifference to federally protected rights.

Enforcement of Antidiscrimination Laws

The Equal Employment Opportunity Commission (EEOC) is the federal agency charged with responsibility for receiving and investigating charges of discrimination arising under Title VII, the ADA, and the ADEA. Before an employee can file suit under those statutes, he or she must first file a discrimination charge with the EEOC (or the state human rights agency) and go through the EEOC process.

The purpose of the EEOC's investigation is to determine whether there is reasonable cause to believe the charge is true. If the EEOC determines that reasonable cause does not exist, it must dismiss the charge and notify the complainant, who nevertheless may file a lawsuit in federal court within 90 days of receiving the EEOC's decision. (This notice is called a right-to-sue letter.) The EEOC's findings are not binding upon the court hearing the lawsuit. A complainant also may request and receive a right-to-sue letter before the EEOC completes its investigation.

If the EEOC determines that there is reasonable cause to support the allegations contained in the charge of discrimination, it must attempt to eliminate the cause of the unlawful practice through conference, conciliation, and persuasion. If conciliation efforts are unsuccessful, the EEOC can file its own suit against the employer, refer the matter to the U.S. Attorney General for civil action, or issue a right-to-sue letter to the complainant.

THE EQUAL PAY ACT OF 1963 (EQUAL PAY ACT)

The Equal Pay Act prohibits differences in pay between men and women for the performance of "substantially equal jobs," unless the differences are due to a factor other than sex, such as a bona fide merit system, training program, or seniority system. "Substantially equal jobs" are those that require equal skills, effort, and responsibility and that are performed under similar working conditions. The Equal Pay Act applies to all employers regardless of the number of their employees.

In contrast to an employee's burden to prove the employer's discriminatory motivation in a Title VII case, the burden falls to the employer in an equal-pay case to prove that some factor other than sex justified the pay disparity between male and female employees holding the same position. An employee who prevails on a claim under the Equal Pay Act may recover back pay in the amount of the wage differential. If the employer's conduct was willful, the court may double the damage award, unless the employer demonstrates that it acted in a sincere and reasonable belief that its conduct was lawful. The back-pay award is generally limited to two years, unless the court determines that the violation was willful, in which case the back pay may be extended to three years. In addition, an award of attorney's fees and costs to the prevailing party is mandatory.

UNIFORMED SERVICES EMPLOYMENT AND REEMPLOYMENT RIGHTS ACT (USERRA)

USERRA provides job and benefit protection for members of the uniformed services, allowing employees to take up to five years of leave without pay to perform military service — and then return to their jobs. USERRA applies to all employers, regardless of size, and prohibits employers from discriminating against employees who are committed to perform military service. Under USERRA, "service" in the uniformed services means "voluntary or involuntary duty in a uniformed service, including active duty, active duty for training, inactive duty training, full-time National Guard duty, or absence for a physical." To enjoy the protection of the Act, employees are required to provide employers advance written or verbal notice of the employee's need for leave (such as a copy of employee's orders).

While USERRA does not require employers to compensate employees on leave for military service, employees qualifying under the Act are entitled to retain their seniority within the company and to enjoy the same benefits provided to employees on other forms of unpaid leave. Employers must provide the option of a COBRA-type of health plan coverage for employees and their eligible dependents while the employee is on military leave. Once an employee's military service is completed, he or she has the right to reinstatement if the employer is notified within a sufficient period of time. That time varies based on the length of the employee's service.

Qualified employees returning from military service generally must be reemployed in the position formerly held or the position the employee would have attained had he been continuously employed. If the returning individual is not qualified, he must be reemployed in the position he left or in a similar position. An employee who is reinstated may be discharged only for "cause" during a defined period of time after he returns to work. The length of the protected employment term, generally 180 days or one year, depends on the amount of time the employee had spent in the military.

Employees and the federal government can sue employers for violations of USERRA. A plaintiff in such a case could obtain compensation for lost wages and benefits, and in the case of willful violations, liquidated damages in an amount equal to the actual damages, plus attorney's fees, expert witness fees, and other litigation costs.

FAMILY AND MEDICAL LEAVE ACT OF 1993 (FMLA)

The federal FMLA requires private sector employers of 50 or more employees at a particular location to provide up to 12 weeks of unpaid leave — during which time his or her job is protected — to eligible employees who have worked for 1,250 hours over the preceding 12 months. FMLA leave is allowed to eligible employees for childbirth and newborn care; adoption; recovery from a serious medical condition; or care of a seriously ill spouse, child, or parent. Some states' laws provide even greater benefits and allowances.

The FMLA is enforced by the U.S. Department of Labor. An employee who is denied leave under the FMLA may file a federal lawsuit to recover monetary damages and equitable relief, including reinstatement and promotion. An employer who violates the FMLA may be held liable for the monetary damages resulting from a violation of the Act. These damages include wages, salary, benefits, or other compensation lost by the employee; monetary damages sustained as a direct result of the violation; as well as attorney's fees, expert witness fees, and other litigation costs. In addition, the amount of recovered damages will be doubled unless the employer can prove that it acted in good faith and reasonably believed that it was not violating the FMLA.

HEALTH INSURANCE PORTABILITY AND ACCOUNTABILITY ACT (HIPAA)

Pursuant to this law enacted in 1996, "privacy standards" regulations, designed to protect individuals' health care information, were adopted in 2003. The privacy standards protect not only written medical records but also health information that is transmitted orally or electronically in any form.

Information is protected if it relates to an individual's health, health care, or payment for health care, and when it identifies or can be used to identify the individual. The protection exists whether the entity creates the information or is the receiver of the information. The privacy standards place controls on an entity's internal use and external disclosures of protected health information.

The privacy standards apply not only to health care providers, but also to most individual or group plans that provide or pay for the cost of medical care. Various tasks performed by a nonprofit's human resources personnel with respect to health benefit plans will involve the flow of protected health information. Some examples include explaining specific benefits under the health plan, verifying coverage for certain procedures, reviewing health care expenses for reimbursement, auditing paid claims to ensure accuracy, and analyzing claims experience.

Human resources personnel play key roles in helping to identify protected health information, both internally and externally. They must determine who are "business associates" subject to formal nondisclosure agreements, and which employees should have access to such information. Orientation of human resources personnel should include training regarding the HIPAA privacy standards. And employee disciplinary policies should cover consequences for improper use and disclosure of protected health information.

Nonprofit organizations should take note that some employment laws will not have direct application unless the organization is of a particular size. For example, the federal Families with Medical Leave Act provisions apply only to organizations that have 50 or more employees. Similarly, state statutory antidiscrimination procedures often apply only to organizations with 15 or more employees. When the employment rules come from county or local jurisdictions, they are more likely to apply to organizations without regard to the number of employees they may have. Notwithstanding these limitations, a prudent board of directors and chief executive will ensure that the organization is compliant with the principles of these employment laws, particularly those regarding employment discrimination and workplace safety, to avoid unnecessary exposure to liability in a civil lawsuit from an aggrieved employee.

COMMON-LAW DOCTRINES AFFECTING THE EMPLOYER-EMPLOYEE RELATIONSHIP

In addition to specific federal and state laws and regulations, several common-law doctrines have altered the traditional principle of employment-at-will. Nonprofit employers should understand the risk and potential consequences of employee claims for breach of contract, wrongful discharge, and violations of certain public policy protections.

BREACH OF CONTRACT ACTIONS

An employment relationship governed by a written contract for a specified duration, or limiting termination to defined causes, is not at-will employment. And in certain cases in which the employer and employee have not actually entered into a written employment agreement, courts have recognized an implied contract. Often these cases involve employee personnel manuals, with the employee claiming that the manual or handbook sufficiently established the conditions of employment to permit the court to find that a contract is implied and to bind the parties by the manual's terms and conditions. An employee manual ought to contain a clear disclaimer of any intent to create an employment contract because some courts will recognize and enforce a disclaimer of this kind.

In addition, employers have been held liable for breaches of verbal promises to applicants or employees. Nonprofit managers should caution supervisors against making statements to employees that could be construed as a promise of continued employment. In turbulent times, employees are likely to seek reassurance about job security. A comment like, "As long as you continue to do a good job, you should be with us for a long time," may pose the risk of a claim for termination in breach of that promise.

The employee personnel manual usually spells out an employer's policies and procedures on matters such as absenteeism, tardiness, leave, discipline, performance, reviews, and various benefits offered to employees. The manual also should clearly state the organization's policies promoting equal opportunity employment and prohibiting workplace harassment. The manual should require the employee's signature acknowledging receipt of the manual and his or her responsibility for following codes of conduct and applicable policies — even though the manual is not a contract.

PUBLIC POLICY PROTECTIONS

The courts in many states have determined that employees should not be terminated for exercising their legal rights and have recognized a cause of action for employees discharged for exercising those rights. These claims often are referred to as public policy exceptions to the at-will employment rule. For example, courts have allowed an employee, terminated for filing a workers' compensation claim permitted by law, to recover for wrongful discharge. Similarly, many states allow employees to recover under common-law or statutory "whistleblower" claims, on proof of an adverse employment action solely because the employee disclosed an unfair or illegal practice by the employer. In addition, courts have recognized a cause of action for wrongful discharge on behalf of an employee who was terminated for refusing to violate a valid law.

TORT CLAIMS

Circumstances may arise where employees claim to have been injured as a result of the wrongful conduct of the nonprofit employer. Employment-related tort claims may include claims for injuries due to employer negligence. In litigation of these claims, a negligence theory may be successfully asserted by the plaintiff when seeking damages against the employer for the negligent hiring, training, retention, or supervision of an employee who has assaulted and injured another employee in the workplace. Negligent-hiring cases arise when a plaintiff maintains that the employer breached its duty to the plaintiff by hiring an employee it knew or should have known had a history of workplace violence or sexual harassment. Under the negligent-retention theory, some courts have held an employer liable if it retained an employee that it knew or should have known posed a threat to other employees.

DEFAMATION AND INTERFERENCE WITH BUSINESS RELATIONS

An employee may also claim to have been defamed by an employer's derogatory statements to a prospective employer. A defamation claim also may arise when an employee claims to have been fired or demoted on the basis of a false accusation by the employer or by another employee. Although the proof requirements vary from state to state, in general, a plaintiff claiming defamation must demonstrate that 1) the defendant made a defamatory statement concerning the plaintiff; 2) the statement was "published," or communicated to others, by the defendant; and 3) the plaintiff was injured by the statement. As a general rule, truth is a defense to a defamation claim.

Interference with business relations is a *business tort* claim that may also come into play in the employer-employee relationship. For example, a former employee may allege that he or she was denied future employment on the basis of conduct or derogatory statements by the former employer. In cases involving references, some courts have held that an employer holds a "conditional privilege" when responding to direct inquiries regarding former employees and may not be held liable for truthful responses, so long as the privilege is not abused.

But to be safest from incurring liability, nonprofit organizations should be careful when responding to inquiries from prospective employers of former employees. All responses should be truthful, fully supportable, and documented. The supervisor giving the reference for the organization should avoid inappropriate or unnecessary characterizations of personal habits of former employees. Some nonprofits ask an employee leaving its employment to designate in writing whether or not he or she wants any information beyond basic employment data provided to prospective future employers and, if so, who on the nonprofit's staff the employee designates to provide a reference.

FRAUD OR MISREPRESENTATION

Liability for a fraud or misrepresentation claim may arise when an employee alleges that he or she was induced to leave a prior job by promises of the new employer, only to find that the promises were not fulfilled by the new employer. A misrepresentation claim also might arise when an employer makes certain promises that persuade an employee to stay, and the employee later finds that they were not fulfilled. Although courts in some states have refused to recognize fraud or misrepresentation claims in the employment context, nonprofits should be aware of this potential source of liability.

TRADE SECRETS AND CONFIDENTIAL INFORMATION

If a nonprofit has important proprietary and confidential information to which an employee will have access, employment contracts and employment policies provide an opportunity to protect that information from disclosure by employees during and following employment. Protected information must be identified specifically so as to give appropriate notice of confidentiality. For example, a nonprofit might consider a contract with its development director that would prohibit the director's future use or disclosure of names and information about the nonprofit's major donors.

PRIVACY CONCERNS

Common and statutory laws in many states impose a wide variety of "privacy" restrictions on employers. These fall into several categories:

- *Discrimination based on personal habits:* Some states restrict the questions an employer may ask about an applicant's off-work activities. For example, it may be unlawful to refuse to hire tobacco smokers or people who drink alcohol on their own time because the state's law may prohibit an employer from refusing to hire a person for engaging in a lawful activity away from work, so long as the activity does not affect the employee's ability to perform his or her duties.

- *Background checks and credit reports:* Some nonprofits want to do thorough background checks on all potential employees. Those organizations must be careful when inquiring into an applicant's criminal record, employment history, or credit history, that those matters relate directly to the specific job being applied for. On the other hand, some organizations never bother to make inquiry into the background or credit of potential employees. Those nonprofits need to be aware that some states place an affirmative duty on certain employers to conduct such investigations if it is foreseeable that a particular type of harm may occur, and if the cost of doing such checks is outweighed by their utility.

What are the legal parameters when investigating an employee's background? Most law applicable to employee criminal background checks derives from state law, and it varies widely from state to state. In most states, the scope of the background check will be dictated, in large part, by the type of job for which the employee is applying and by the exposure to liability that an employee's job represents to the employer. Generally (and unless state law precludes it), an employer is free to ask an applicant if he or she has any convictions for felonies or misdemeanors on a job application, and whether the nonprofit can contact past employers to discuss the employee. In Maryland, for example, an employer is free to inquire as to an employee's criminal background, and is only limited in that the employer cannot demand that an employee disclose criminal charges that have been expunged from his record. On the other hand, Massachusetts law allows a person to apply for a job without revealing anything about his criminal record.

Each nonprofit must ascertain from legal counsel what restrictions or requirements are placed on it relative to inquiring about employees' backgrounds. Then employers must be consistent and thorough when conducting criminal background checks. Otherwise, the employer may be found liable for negligently failing to discover the criminal background of an employee *after* the employee has exposed the employer to substantial liability.

Background checks on potential employees are also usually permitted to explore integrity and financial stability. While credit checks are generally permitted, significant restrictions are placed on them by both the federal and state law. The federal Fair Credit Reporting Act (FCRA), for example, requires that employers notify an applicant or employee that a consumer report may be obtained about that person for employment purposes. The employer must obtain written permission from the employee before getting the report, and must provide the employee with a written description of rights under the FCRA (including contesting the report) before any adverse employment action can be taken based on the results. Typically, employers request an employee's permission at the time of hiring and as a condition of employment.

- *Employee expectations of privacy:* In some circumstances, common and statutory law may give employees a reasonable expectation of privacy with respect to personal information in the workplace. This expectation of privacy can arise in the context of medical information, workplace searches, video surveillance, and monitoring computer or Internet use. For example, the Americans with Disabilities Act and the Family and Medical Leave Act impose certain record-keeping and information-sharing provisions on employers with respect to employee medical conditions and accommodations. The ADA and FMLA require employers to keep employee medical information confidential and in files separate from their personnel files. Employers may disclose such information, however, to those who may need to know about an employee's condition. Examples of individuals who may need to know include supervisors, managers, first-aid and safety personnel, and government officials investigating compliance.

Federal and state laws also limit the extent to which employers can monitor the activities of employees in certain circumstances. Employers must comply with federal and state statutes that govern the monitoring of telephone calls, e-mail, Internet use, and other forms of communication. Under the Electronic Communications Privacy Act (ECPA), employers are prohibited from intercepting or disclosing the contents of an electronic, oral, or wire communication. Employers are also prohibited from accessing wire and electronic communications in electronic storage without proper authorization. There are exceptions to the pro-hibition on interceptions, such as when employees provide consent to intercept communications. Many nonprofits have specific policies in their employee personnel manuals making it clear that all electronic communications utilizing employer's equipment are the property of the employer and making an employee's consent to examination of those communications a condition of employment.

Employers should develop policies that govern employees' use of equipment — particularly electronic equipment — and other workplace activities. Establishing appropriate policies and practices in writing can reduce a nonprofit's exposure to invasion of privacy claims. In addition, such policies will help employers monitor their employees' activities and protect confidential and proprietary information.

With respect to common-law claims, each state has its own body of case law when determining whether and to what extent an employer may intrude on private or personal information. Generally, employers should not unreasonably intrude on employees when employees have a reasonable expectation of privacy. An employee's reasonable expectation of privacy is usually based on the facts and circumstances of a particular case. For example, videotaping employees in changing areas or where medical exams are conducted would likely intrude on an employee's right to privacy — whereas videotaping common areas of the workplace may be perfectly acceptable.

- *Polygraph restrictions:* The use of "lie detector" tests in the workplace presents a special issue. The Employee Polygraph Protection Act (EPPA) prohibits employers from requiring, requesting, suggesting, or causing any employee or prospective employee to submit to a lie detector test. It also forbids employers from using, accepting, referring to, or inquiring about the results of a lie detector test voluntarily taken by any employee or prospective employee. An employer cannot discharge, discipline, discriminate against in any manner, deny employment or promotion to, or threaten to take action against any employee or prospective employee who refuses to take a lie detector test, or based on the results of any lie detector test. The employee's rights under the act may not be waived by contract. An employer may not disclose the results of a lie detector test except to the examinee, a court or similar body, or to a government agency, insofar as the disclosed information is an admission of criminal conduct.

VIOLENCE IN THE WORKPLACE

As a general rule, employers are not liable for the violent acts of their employees unless the acts are related to job duties or the employer could have reasonably foreseen that an employee was likely to commit a violent act. A violent incident in the workplace may lead to claims that an employer negligently hired, retained, or supervised the employee who committed the violent act or did not take due care to maintain a safe environment. Whether an employer will be held liable depends on whether it had reason to know that an employee had a propensity toward violence and, if so, by what means the employer attempted to protect fellow employees from the violent employee. In addition to background checks, an employer's protections against workplace violence should include proper security for its employees, visitors, and clients, and effective policies that prohibit any harassment, intimidation, or threats of violence. The organization should also inform all employees that it has a zero-tolerance policy towards threat of violence in the workplace.

ARBITRATION OF WORKPLACE DISPUTES

In an effort to curb the costs of litigation with employees, some nonprofit employers have adopted arbitration plans as an alternative to resolve disputes with employees. The U.S. Supreme Court has held that arbitration clauses are enforceable and can be used to settle employees' claims against employers, including statutory discrimination claims. (However, once a charge of discrimination is filed with the EEOC, that agency is in control of the process and an employer may still have to satisfy its obligations under the administrative process.)

New employees can be required to arbitrate claims as a condition of their employment and existing employees, if necessary, can be requested to agree to arbitration of any claims, as well. Arbitration agreements cannot, of course, attempt to obtain employees' consent to restrictions of their rights or contain unconscionable provisions.

Whether or not to adopt an arbitration policy will often depend on practical workplace considerations. For example, employers with few or no employee claims may not want to upset the good morale of employees. Conversely, employers with a history of workplace disputes may find it cost-effective to adopt such a provision.

CHAPTER Q&As

Q: Does our chief executive officer need a written employment agreement?

A: If a chief executive officer does not have a written employment agreement, the law considers the chief executive to be serving "at will," meaning he or she can quit at any time and the employer can likewise exercise its discretion to terminate the relationship at any time. An at-will employment relationship can be terminated by either party for any reason or for no reason at all. In most cases, because of the importance of the chief executive to the achievement of the organization's mission, the parties will wish to specify the terms of the chief executive's employment in a written agreement. Important provisions will include the specific duties required of the chief executive, the term of the agreement, the compensation and benefits of the chief executive, the ability of the organization to terminate the chief executive with or without cause, the organization's obligations to reimburse the expenses of the chief executive, and whether the chief executive will serve on the organization's board of directors with or without a vote.

The board should consider entering into a written employment agreement with its chief executive, and with other senior management where warranted. The board will need to ensure that it has conducted appropriate due diligence in determining the chief executive's compensation and that adequate supporting documentation is placed into the files. In light of recent corporate scandals, the board chair should ensure that the process of determining the chief executive's compensation and benefits is conducted with the active participation of the full board.

Q: Do the employment laws apply to our volunteers?

A: For the most part, these laws are intended to protect employees of an organization and do not have direct application to volunteers. However, some workplace laws will have direct or indirect application to volunteers, such as those laws mandating workplace safety. It is also important to be certain whether a particular individual is a volunteer for these purposes. For example, a volunteer who receives a stipend to assist with living expenses may end up being characterized as an employee rather than as a volunteer, thereby bringing him or her within the protections of these laws.

Employees and volunteers are the lifeblood of a nonprofit organization. They are individuals dedicated to fulfilling the organization's vital mission, often for salary and benefits that are less than those received by their colleagues at for-profit organizations. Employers are subject to increased regulation by the federal and state government regarding employee hours in wages, discrimination, discipline, family and medical leave, and employee disabilities. They are held responsible for ensuring basic workplace safety and employees' security. Most recently, they must maintain a delicate balance between monitoring employee behavior on behalf of the organization and maintaining employee privacy. As result of this high degree of regulation, directors must be familiar with the basic principles of these rules as set out in this chapter. The board must ensure that the organization consistently applies its personnel policies.

QUESTIONS THE BOARD SHOULD ASK

- Is the board confident that payroll taxes are paid every year without fail?

- Does the board review the personnel manual from time to time?

- Does our organization have a clear understanding on the rules differentiating between employees and independent contractors?

- Should we consider a policy of mediation or arbitration of employee claims?

- Do we have suitable records retention practices?

- Do we have adequate controls in place to protect confidential and private information?

7.
Employee Benefits Law

John C. Baldwin

Initially, it should be stated that a nonprofit employer is not required to provide any benefits to its employees, aside from salary or wages. Any additional benefits are purely voluntary on the part of the nonprofit. However, in today's environment, a nonprofit may have a very hard time attracting and retaining competent employees unless it offers some minimum level of benefits, such as medical insurance and a retirement plan.

Due to the complexity of employee benefit laws, it is common and likely necessary for the board of directors and management to rely upon the advice of experts in the field. Thus, the board may wish to retain a knowledgeable outside attorney, an actuary, or an accounting firm for general planning purposes. These consultants should be familiar with plan options that are appropriate for the organization and that are safely in compliance with the law. The board should obtain legal counsel experienced in this area to review the plans proposed for adoption and to make necessary regulatory filings. Occasionally, an organization will be contacted by federal regulators, such as the IRS or the Department of Labor, regarding the organization's employee benefit plans. In such cases, the organization should promptly consult legal counsel to assess the situation and to make an appropriate response.

The board of directors is ultimately responsible for ensuring that any benefit plans the organization provides to its employees are in compliance with the law and that funding for such plans has been secured in a prudent manner and with prudent investments. The organization risks liability for claims made by aggrieved employees in the event of a failure of such a plan, and if the directors were found to be negligent in their actions, they risk exposure to personal liability.

If a nonprofit chooses to offer benefits, then it becomes subject to federal employee benefit law — whether it is a small operation with one or two paid staff or a university or hospital that is the largest employer in its community. Under federal law, employee benefits are divided into two categories:

1. pension benefit plans, and

2. welfare benefit plans.

Both types of plans are governed by the landmark federal Employee Retirement Income Security Act of 1974 (ERISA).

Under ERISA, an employee *pension benefit plan* ("pension plan") is a plan maintained by an employer that provides retirement income to employees or results in a deferral of income by employees.

An employee *welfare benefit plan* ("welfare plan") is any plan maintained by an employer that provides participating employees and (or) their beneficiaries with medical, surgical, or hospital benefits; vacation benefits; apprenticeship programs; prepaid legal services; benefits in the event of sickness, accident, disability, or death; or other similar benefits (but not retirement income).

Pension Benefit Plans

As noted above, *pension plan* is a generic term for any plan that provides retirement income. There are two general categories of pension plans: *qualified* and *nonqualified*. Most retirement plans sponsored by employers for the benefit of employees are qualified plans, which means that the plan is written and administered in compliance with the voluminous requirements in the Internal Revenue Code. For example, a qualified pension plan must comply with minimum requirements on eligibility, vesting (nonforfeitability), distributions, forms of benefit payment, funding, and nondiscrimination.

The hallmark of a qualified plan is that it must not discriminate — either as written or in operation — in favor of employees identified as "highly compensated employees." Therefore, a qualified plan may not cover highly compensated employees while excluding non–highly compensated employees. Likewise, the benefits provided under the plan must not be disproportionately greater for highly compensated employees than for non–highly compensated employees.

A nonqualified plan, on the other hand, is also designed to provide retirement income, but it need not comply with the minimum requirements in the Internal Revenue Code for qualified plans. A qualified plan will cover most or all employees; a nonqualified plan can be used by an employer to provide deferred compensation to senior executives or key employees. While a qualified plan must cover many employees to avoid illegal discrimination, a nonqualified plan can be limited to a single employee. An employer can establish one nonqualified plan for some or all of its executives or it could establish a separate nonqualified plan for each of its executives.

Besides the ability to discriminate in favor of executive and highly compensated employees, the nonqualified plan is also treated differently with respect to vesting (nonforfeitability) of benefits. Under a qualified plan, benefits that become vested are nevertheless not subject to income tax until the benefit is paid out to the participant or his or her beneficiary. With a nonqualified plan, however, benefits are taxable as soon as they are no longer subject to a substantial risk of forfeiture (i.e., as soon as they are vested), regardless of whether the benefit has been distributed by the plan.

Another difference between qualified and nonqualified plans exists with respect to rollovers. Benefits distributed in a lump sum from a qualified plan may be rolled over on a tax-free basis into a plan of a new employer or into an individual retirement account. Benefits distributed from a nonqualified plan are not eligible for such rollover treatment.

There are a number of different types of pension plans, both qualified and non-qualified.

Examples of Qualified Retirement Plans

1. *Defined Benefit Pension Plan:* This plan is the old-style pension plan favored in the past by large employers, such as hospitals. The plan does not have individual employee accounts, but has a benefit formula based upon the individual's compensation and years of service. A typical formula might be 2 percent of final compensation multiplied by total years of service. Employer

contributions are determined each year by the plan actuary, based upon assumptions regarding salary levels, interest rates, mortality, and turnover. With a defined benefit plan, the economic risk is with the employer. The benefit formula is in the nature of a promise to the participant, and the employer must contribute over time whatever amount is actuarially necessary to meet that promise. Because of this, very few employers are adopting new defined benefit plans, and many existing defined benefit plans are being converted into cash balance plans for reasons of cost containment. Benefits under a defined benefit plan are insured in part by an agency of the federal government known as the Pension Benefit Guaranty Corporation.

2. *Defined Contribution Pension Plan:* This type of plan is based on an individual account for each participant and contains a specific contribution formula, for example, 8 percent of annual compensation to be contributed each year. This type of plan is easier for employees to understand and no actuary is needed to calculate the annual contribution. However, the required contribution must be made by the employer each year and there is very little flexibility. Unlike the defined benefit plan, the participant (not the employer) bears the consequences of negative investment results — but he also gains the benefit of positive investment results. The benefit ultimately payable to a participant depends upon the annual contributions and the investment returns for the plan over the number of years of participation. Benefits under this type of plan are not insured by the Pension Benefit Guaranty Corporation.

3. *Profit Sharing Plan:* This type of plan is similar to a defined contribution pension plan, except that a profit sharing plan need not have a specific contribution that must be met every year. A profit sharing plan typically provides for an annual discretionary contribution, giving flexibility to the employer to determine whether a contribution will be made and the amount of such contribution, which can fluctuate from year to year. Although nonprofits do not technically have any "profits" to share with employees, they are nevertheless eligible to establish a profit sharing plan.

4. *401(k) Plan:* This is also known as a "cash or deferred arrangement." It gives participating employees the right to elect to defer some of their income into the plan — but only before that income is earned. The employee election may be based upon current compensation levels (limited to compensation not yet earned) or the employer may contribute its own dollars, giving the employee a choice between receiving current cash or a greater contribution and benefit under the plan. Each participating employee will make his or her own election by executing a salary reduction agreement. In today's cost-conscious world, 401(k) plans are probably the most popular retirement plan for nonprofit employers to establish because they do not require a contribution by the employer.

EXAMPLES OF NONQUALIFIED RETIREMENT PLANS

1. *Tax-Sheltered Annuity Plan (TSA):* The Section 403(b) annuity provides retirement income for employees of tax-exempt Section 501(c)(3) nonprofit organizations and of public schools. These are individual account, defined contribution plans, which may be funded with a combination of employee salary reduction contributions and new dollars, which are contributed by the

employer. These annuity contract plans are typically operated by or in conjunction with large insurance companies.

2. *Section 457 Deferred Compensation Plans:* This type of plan can be adopted by any organization that is exempt from tax. Such plans are specifically for the benefit of executives and key employees and are in increasing use as a method by which a nonprofit can retain those important employees. In general, these plans have the benefit of being exempt from many requirements that apply to qualified plans, including exemption from the vesting, funding, and fiduciary requirements of ERISA. They also have a disadvantage, in that the plan's obligation to pay money to the employee at a later date must remain unsecured in order for the employee to avoid constructive receipt of income for tax purposes. Therefore, the employee participant is technically just another unsecured general creditor of the employer. A way to avoid this drawback is for the employer to set money aside for these employees through the use of an irrevocable trust.

WELFARE BENEFIT PLANS

According to ERISA, a welfare benefit plan does not provide retirement income, but instead provides any of the following: medical, surgical, or hospital benefits; benefits in the event of sickness, accident, disability, death, or unemployment; vacation benefits; apprenticeship training programs; daycare centers; scholarship funds; or prepaid legal services. Minimal welfare benefit plans offered by most nonprofit employers include health care, group life insurance, and long-term disability. As with pension benefit plans, the requirements of ERISA must be met in order for a nonprofit to operate the plan within the law.

Welfare benefit plans are not required to provide for any vesting whatsoever. Employers have the right to terminate welfare benefits, and to cut back on the level of existing benefits without regard to the concept of vesting as it applies to pension plans.

While health care benefits do not become vested, however, certain employees, former employees, and their dependents who experience a "qualifying event" have rights under ERISA to "continuation coverage" for a period between 18 and 36 months — as long as the covered individual continues to pay the premiums. It should also be noted that a health care benefit plan is a "covered entity" under the Health Insurance Portability and Accountability Act (HIPAA), requiring a nonprofit to observe the privacy rules and information security standards set forth in that law.

Welfare benefit plans have been funded historically by group insurance contracts issued by insurance carriers. As the cost of health care has risen, however, many larger nonprofits have found it economically beneficial to fund the cost of welfare benefits through a tax-exempt trust, known as a voluntary employees' beneficiary association (VEBA) under Section 501(c)(9) of the Internal Revenue Code. A VEBA is expressly permitted to provide for the payment of life, sickness, and accident benefits. Other benefits may be funded through a VEBA, if they are sufficiently similar to life, sickness, and accident benefits. In order for the provision of benefits through a VEBA to be an economically viable option, an organization should have at least 500 employees.

What is the possible benefit of a VEBA to a nonprofit and its employees? As a tax-exempt trust, a VEBA may not seek profits for shareholders — in contrast to for-profit insurance companies, which price their products in the hopes of making a profit for the company and its shareholders. A VEBA's independent actuary, however, prices the cost of benefits with the goal of keeping the welfare benefit plans properly funded, in the best interest of plan participants, beneficiaries, and dependents.

ERISA REQUIREMENTS FOR ALL FUNDED BENEFIT PLANS

FIDUCIARY RESPONSIBILITY

The fiduciary responsibility requirements of ERISA apply to all benefit plans (both pension and welfare plans) other than unfunded deferred compensation plans for the benefit of executives or highly compensated employees. These rules lie at the core of why Congress enacted ERISA in 1974.

Who is a "fiduciary" under ERISA? The plan administrator, the plan trustee, and the plan investment manager of an employee benefit plan are all considered fiduciaries because they possess discretionary authority and (or) discretionary control in the administration of the plan, or they have authority or control in the management or disposition of the plan's assets. The key word here is "discretionary." Individuals or institutions that merely take direction from others and have no discretion are not fiduciaries.

The plan's fiduciaries owe a duty to plan participants and beneficiaries. Plan assets must never inure to the benefit of any employer and must be held for the exclusive purposes of providing benefits to participants and their beneficiaries and for defraying reasonable expenses of the plan's administration. All plan fiduciaries must act in accordance with the plan document, as long as the plan document is consistent with the terms of ERISA.

The key fiduciary standard under ERISA is known as the "prudent man standard of care." Under this standard, a fiduciary must discharge his or her duties with the care, skill, prudence, and diligence, under the circumstances then prevailing that a prudent person acting in a like capacity and familiar with such matters would use in the conduct of an enterprise of a like character and with like aims. The board's responsibility in this regard is to carefully select members of the board to serve as fiduciaries of the retirement plan. Ideally, these will be individuals with some financial acumen and the ability to make a time commitment to the process. The board will retain ongoing responsibility for overseeing the performance of the plan fiduciaries.

The role of fiduciary is not one for inexperienced amateurs, no matter how well intentioned. A plan fiduciary who breaches any of the responsibilities or duties imposed on him is personally liable to make good to the plan any losses that result from the breach, and to give over to the plan any profits earned through the improper use of plan assets. The fiduciary may also be removed from his position, and is subject to possible prosecution by the U.S. Department of Labor.

ENFORCEMENT OF THE PLAN

One result of the increasing efforts by employers and providers to contain health care costs has been an explosion of litigation over benefit plans that shows no sign of abating soon. A plan participant or beneficiary must look to ERISA as the exclusive means of seeking to remedy an alleged wrongful denial of benefits or an alleged breach of fiduciary duty. ERISA supercedes any and all state laws insofar as they relate to any employee benefit plan. ERISA allows a plan participant or beneficiary to bring a lawsuit against a benefit plan to recover benefits under the plan or to clarify rights to future benefits under the plan. Before bringing a lawsuit, the participant is required to exhaust the administrative remedies available to him or her under the employee benefit plan and ERISA.

REPORTING AND DISCLOSURE

ERISA contains very specific requirements for reporting information to the federal government and for disclosing information to plan participants. Disclosure to plan participants is centered on the summary plan description (SPD) described above. ERISA sets forth a detailed list of information that must be included in the SPD, all of which must be presented in nontechnical language. The SPD must be furnished to each participant covered under the plan and to each beneficiary receiving benefits under the plan. The precise content of the SPD need not be reviewed by the government and the SPD need not be filed with the government.

Care must be taken, however, in preparation of the SPD because if the SPD erroneously contains substantive terms that are different from the actual plan document, then the courts may well award the participants whichever of the terms are better for them. Courts have given participants the benefit of better SPD benefit terms, even where the SPD states that in the event of a conflict, the terms of the plan will govern.

While the SPD need not be filed with the government, it is necessary for the plan administrator to file an annual report each year for most employee benefit plans. The annual filing must be made on a Form 5500 Annual Return/Report of Employee Benefit Plan, including various statements and schedules, and possibly including an independent accountant's report, depending upon the type of plan and the number of individuals covered. If the plan is a pension plan subject to the minimum funding rules, then a schedule must also be completed and executed by the plan actuary and attached as part of the form. After the form is filed with the federal government, plan information is shared by the Internal Revenue Service and the Department of Labor.

THE STRUCTURE OF BENEFIT PLANS

Legally, an employee benefit plan is an entity separate from the sponsoring employer, in the same way that a corporation is a separate legal entity. It has its own tax identification number and files its own tax returns.

The money necessary to provide welfare benefits is sometimes provided through a trust or a group insurance contract (that is, a long-term disability contract or a group life insurance contract with an insurance company). If a benefit plan is separately "funded" by such an insurance contract or by a trust, then the assets of the benefit plan and the assets of the sponsoring employer must never be commingled and must always be the subject of separate accounting.

An employee benefit plan generally includes all of the following components:

1. A **plan document** spelling out the benefits, rights, and obligations provided under the plan, and setting forth eligibility requirements that must be met in order for an employee to participate and earn a benefit. The plan document also provides for financial contributions to the plan by the employer, possibly by the employees, or by both.

2. A **trust agreement** establishing the terms under which financial contributions to the plan will be held and invested by the trustee of the plan, pending distribution from the trust to provide benefits established under the plan document.

3. A **sponsoring employer** that has the responsibility for establishing the plan and its content under the law. The sponsoring employer decides if it will have a plan or plans, and if so, the benefits to be provided under the plan, consistent with the requirements of ERISA. The sponsoring employer also has the right to amend the plan and to terminate the plan, again consistent with requirements of ERISA. All of these choices are known as "settlor functions." They are business decisions by the employer, rather than fiduciary decisions.

4. A **plan administrator** who is the person or committee named in the plan document to have the responsibility for ensuring that the terms of the plan are followed. The plan administrator is considered to be a "fiduciary" under ERISA. Some plan sponsors will hire an outside third-party administrator to administer a plan; other plan sponsors will entrust that responsibility to their department of human resources. If the plan document does not designate a plan administrator, then ERISA provides that the plan sponsor itself will also be the plan administrator.

5. A **plan trustee** that holds the plan assets in trust under the terms of the trust agreement and consistent with the plan document. The trustee disburses plan assets to provide benefits at the direction of the plan administrator. The trustee holds and manages plan assets, but does not administer the plan. The trustee may be one or more individuals or may be an institution such as a bank or trust company. As an alternative, the plan assets may be held by an insurance company under a group insurance contract, in which case there may not be a trustee.

6. If the plan has an **investment manager**, then that entity is either a registered investment adviser, a bank, or an insurance company that has the power to manage plan assets, and has acknowledged in writing that it is a plan fiduciary. If the plan has an investment manager, then the plan trustee is not responsible for management of the assets under the control of the investment manager. While a plan may have an investment adviser, that entity may or may not be an investment manager.

7. A **plan participant** is an employee or former employee of the sponsoring employer who is or may become eligible to receive a benefit from an employee benefit plan. In many cases, an employee will need to meet a minimum age and (or) minimum length-of-service requirement before becoming a plan participant.

8. A **beneficiary** is a person designated by a participant or by the terms of the plan document to receive benefits, either now or in the future. In the case of a pension plan, the beneficiary of any death benefit will almost always be the surviving spouse. In the case of a health care benefit plan, the beneficiaries will typically include all members of the participant's immediate family.

9. A **summary plan description** (SPD) summarizing the plan document that is written in nontechnical language so that it gives the average plan participant and the average beneficiary an accurate and comprehensive summary of his or her rights and obligations under the plan. ERISA requires that all participants be given an SPD and that an updated SPD be provided every few years.

10. The **Form 5500** is the annual information return filed with the federal government every year on behalf of most employee benefit plans. Information contained on the return will typically be shared between the Internal Revenue Service and the Department of Labor, both of which have the authority to audit the return to determine whether the plan is being administered as required by law.

CHAPTER Q&As

Q: What is the difference between a "qualified" pension plan and a "nonqualified" plan?

A: A pension plan is a plan that provides retirement income for an organization's employees. There are two general categories of such plans: "qualified" and "non-qualified." Most retirement plans sponsored by nonprofit employers for the benefit of their employees are qualified plans, which means that they're written and administered in compliance with the voluminous requirements of the Internal Revenue Code. The hallmark of a qualified plan is that it may not discriminate in favor of highly compensated employees. The nonqualified plan, on the other hand, is also designed to provide retirement income, but it need not comply with the minimum requirements established by law for qualified plans. Thus, the nonqualified plan can be used by an employer to provide deferred compensation to senior executives or key employees. The taxation and vesting of benefits varies between plans as well. Under a qualified plan, benefits that become vested are not taxed until the benefit is paid out to the participant. With a nonqualified plan, however, benefits are taxable as soon as they are vested regardless of whether the benefit has been actually distributed by the plan.

Q: What is the difference between a pension plan and a welfare benefit plan?

A: A pension plan is a generic term for any plan that provides retirement income. Examples include defined benefit plans, defined contribution plans, profit sharing plans, 401(k) plans, tax-sheltered annuity plans, and section 457 plans. A welfare benefit plan does not provide retirement income, but instead provides any of the following: medical, surgical, or hospital benefits; benefits in the event of sickness, accident, disability, death, or unemployment; vacation benefits; apprenticeship training programs; daycare centers; scholarship funds; or prepaid legal services. Minimal welfare benefit plans offered by most nonprofit employers include health care, group life insurance, and long-term disability.

An essential factor in recruiting and retaining good management and staff in a nonprofit organization is the availability of appropriate and competitive employee benefit programs. The chief executive officer and directors must keep apprised of the different types of pension plan options available to nonprofit organizations. These rules change frequently, and the diligent chief executive will consult with financial advisers and counsel to determine which plans are most effective and which may have become obsolete. In particular, the chief executive and the board must be wary of pension plan strategies peddled by aggressive consultants that are "too good to be true." The consequences for the organization of adopting a pension plan that is later found to be in violation of law can be disastrous both financially and for employee morale. The board must also show caution when considering the long-term financial consequences of adopting a particular pension plan for the organization. This is an extremely complex area of the law and reliance on good outside counsel is necessary. However, the board must carefully exercise its duty of due care to question reports of its consultants to ensure that they are reliable. The board and the chief executive will also need to work diligently to stay informed of employee welfare benefit plans that will satisfy the needs of workers without placing the organization at financial risk.

QUESTIONS THE BOARD SHOULD ASK

- Do we have clear objectives for our employee benefits philosophy?

- Do we have someone verifying that we are in compliance with all the applicable laws governing our organization?

- On our Form 990, do we report total compensation accurately and not only salary data?

8.
Immigration Law

Geoffrey S. Tobias

In the 21st century, nonprofit organizations are, of necessity, taking a more global outlook in their operations. Employees, volunteers, and board members are now drawn from an international pool, even within rural communities. At the same time, they operate in a world that is caught up in a war against terror. The federal government, in particular, has imposed restrictions on interactions with foreigners that mandate fundamental changes in the way organizations deal with them. As a result, directors and chief executive officers must now pay attention to a body of law they may have rarely considered in the past: immigration law.

Some nonprofit organizations will have a greater need to be diligent in this area and to keep board members informed. Health care organizations have for years recruited foreign medical graduates to provide needed medical services in the community. They are largely accustomed to dealing with the visa requirements for these professionals. However, they will need to stay on top of changing rules and the timing exigencies that result from the limitations set by the government on various visa categories. Colleges and universities also frequently hire foreign nationals to teach and perform research and they may conduct foreign student exchange programs. They too will need to remain vigilant in working with counsel and consultants in ensuring their compliance with the immigration laws. Directors should ensure that the chief executive and the human relations staff have procedures in place for verifying the immigration status of foreigners involved in the organization's operations and programs. This is in addition to the longstanding requirement of an I-9 being completed for *all* new hires.

In all of these instances, a nonprofit will encounter the arcane world of U.S. immigration law. Noncitizens coming to the United States are today subject to increased scrutiny at the U.S. border and beyond. For these and other reasons, a nonprofit wishing to employ or serve noncitizens must be aware of the basic structure of immigration law.

Every noncitizen entering the United States must be granted a visa by a consular officer of the United States at more than 200 consulates throughout the world, or must be coming as a visitor from certain visa waiver countries. While in many circumstances the U.S. Citizenship and Immigration Service (CIS) determines whether a person is eligible for a nonimmigrant status, the Consul in the noncitizen's home country has the final say as to whether the visa will be granted. Once the visa is granted, by imprinting a machine-readable document (with photograph) in the noncitizen's passport, he or she can be accepted for transportation to the United States by a commercial carrier. At the U.S. border (typically an international airport), the noncitizen must present his or her visa to a CIS officer, who makes the ultimate decision as to whether the person will be admitted to the United States.

Once in the United States, it is possible to apply for a change of status from the CIS, which approves all changes of status from one nonimmigrant classification to another. For example, a noncitizen who originally was granted a student visa and entered as a student, may often wish to change status to an H-1 "specialized worker." If the non-citizen remains in the United States in the new status, there is nothing further to be done with regard to the now-obsolete student visa. However, on the noncitizen's very first departure from the United States, he or she must visit a U.S. Consul and have the new visa imprinted in the passport. That is, once one changes nonimmigrant status, it is essential to have a new visa imprinted in the passport prior to returning to the United States.

The most fundamental distinction in U.S. immigration law is between two broad categories — nonimmigrants and immigrants.

NONIMMIGRANT STATUS

Often nonimmigrant status may be obtained by an applicant much more quickly and easily than that of immigrant, so examination of the best route for a noncitizen entering the United States for nonprofit employment usually begins with nonimmigrant requirements. (And, in fact, the two are not mutually exclusive: Non-immigrant status can be obtained and serve as the basis for employment while the lengthier permanent residency process is pursued.)

VISITOR VISAS, B-1 AND B-2

By far the largest number of visas (or visa waivers) issued are "B-1" business visitors or "B-2" visitors for pleasure. B visas are granted directly by a U.S. Consul (except in the case of visa waiver countries). The basic requirements are that the noncitizen must show a *bona fide* intent to depart from the United States after a relatively short and definable stay, that the person has contacts in his or her own country, and that adequate financial arrangements have been made to support the noncitizen during the temporary stay.

COUNTRIES OF DEPARTURE THAT DO NOT REQUIRE VISAS BEFORE ENTERING THE UNITED STATES

Andorra	France	Luxembourg	Singapore
Australia	Germany	Monaco	Slovenia
Austria	Iceland	Netherlands	Spain
Belgium	Ireland	New Zealand	Sweden
Brunei	Italy	Norway	Switzerland
Denmark	Japan	Portugal	United Kingdom
Finland	Liechtenstein	San Marino	Uruguay

The majority of B nonimmigrants now enter the United States pursuant to visa waivers.

Visa waiver nonimmigrants are granted a 90-day stay in the United States. Generally, the only documents one needs to possess is a passport and return airfare. Visa waiver entrants are usually not quizzed too intently with regard to the purpose of their trip. But the *quid pro quo* for the benefit of not having to apply for a visa with a consul is that visa waiver entrants cannot extend their stay beyond 90 days (except in emergency situations), and they may not change their nonimmigrant status from B to any other nonimmigrant or immigrant status.

Canadian citizens have never been required to have a visa and may enter the United States as visitors upon presentation of a passport, driver's license, or other suitable identification. Note that many immigration inspectors are quite adept at discovering an intent to visit the United States that is inconsistent with visitor status.

Business visitors (B-1) cannot be employed in the United States, either as employees or as independent contractors. Moreover, the business visit should relate to his or her foreign employer's business, and compensation paid to the business visitor should be by the employer.

The State Department has issued a list of acceptable B-1 business activities, which give some idea of what is contemplated by the category. For example, employees coming to the United States to solicit sales, negotiate contracts, or take orders for a foreign company are *bona fide* B-1 business visitors. In addition, business visitors may come to the United States with regard to contracts already extant, again remembering that the benefit must accrue to the foreign company. Other acceptable B-1 activities include consultation with U.S. business associates, visits for litigation, attending professional or business conferences and conventions, and coming to the United States for the purpose of conducting research. Professionals or specialized workers seeking to come to the United States as H-1 employees (discussed below) may utilize the business visitor category to seek employment in the United States. Similarly, investors, traders, or intracompany transferees coming to the United States to set up a business may be accorded B-1 status. Other accepted uses of the B-1 visa include coming to attend board of directors' meetings and academic activities where an honorarium will be paid (there are detailed rules on that subcategory).

While traditionally nonwaiver business visitors were granted 90 days in the United States, since 2002, border agents have been quizzing B-1 business visitors intently as to the purpose, duration, and other details of their stays in the United States and limiting the length of visits to as little as 10 days. While the initial stay can be extended (by filing Form I-539), if the visitor entered under a visa and not as a visa waiver, he or she will have to make a further application to the BCIS (see below).

The other frequently used category for noncitizens is the B-2 visitor-for-pleasure status. In addition to the obvious tourist uses, noncitizens may obtain B-2 status to come to the United States for medical treatment (along with household members of the person seeking medical treatment). The key requirements are return airfare, a reasonable itinerary, and sufficient funds to pay for the stay and activities in the United States.

STUDENTS, F STATUS

Full-time noncitizen students in the United States are accorded an "F" status. This applies to elementary through postdoctoral students. No preapproval from the CIS is required. The foreign student obtains an I-20 certificate of eligibility from the school's foreign student advisor (FSA), presents this to the consul along with evidence of support, and is then admitted for the length of time needed to complete the studies.

As you might imagine, F visas are not granted for public elementary and secondary schools unless arrangement for payment has been made.

The student must be enrolled for at least 12 hours, have demonstrated some English proficiency or be taking courses to reach proficiency, and must show that he or she has a true residence abroad that is not being abandoned.

Student noncitizens rarely require much in the way of legal assistance, inasmuch as college FSAs are quite proficient in complying with the law. Subsequent to 9/11, a new Student and Exchange Visitor Information System (SEVIS) has imposed new reporting obligations on schools and students, who must follow precisely the guidance of their FSAs.

In addition to studies, the FSA at the college or university is empowered to grant "work authorization" to students. In this way, noncitizen students can work, part time, as a means of gaining experience. Upon graduation (whether or not the student worked for an employer previously), the FSA may grant "practical training" to the student in two six-month segments. With this, a former student, directly out of college, may work for one year. (And during that year, the employer can decide whether the additional investment of petitioning for H-1 status is worthwhile.)

Since 9/11, the CIS has restricted the relatively open F category, prohibiting would-be students from entering the United States with easily obtained B-2 visitor visas, enrolling in school, and then changing their status to F.

Note that all of the forms referred to herein may be downloaded from the CIS Web site, http://uscis.gov/graphics/formfee/index.htm. The basic forms for applying for a visa, the DS156 and DS157, are available on the Department of State Web site, www.travel.state.gov.

PROFESSIONALS, H-1B STATUS

Possibly the most useful category to many nonprofits is the H-1B "specialized knowledge" status. In order to qualify for such a visa, the noncitizen must have a four-year college degree and be coming to the United States to fill a position requiring the specialized knowledge reflected in the degree. Unfortunately, Congress has limited the availability of H-1B visas to 65,000 (in FY2005), resulting in the quota being filled on the first day of the fiscal year, October 1, 2004. However, on December 8, 2004, an extra 20,000 visas were granted for those earning a master's degree or higher from a U.S. school.

To comply with H-1B requirements, a nonprofit must go through the following steps:

- First, the employer must demonstrate that the position itself requires a four-year degree or its equivalent (which in many cases in the business world is no easy task), and that other persons filling the same type of job for the nonprofit employer are similarly qualified college graduates.

- Then, the nonprofit must determine whether the noncitizen possesses the equivalent of a four-year degree, *in a related field*. If the noncitizen graduated from an accredited U.S. institution, you need go no further. If the noncitizen graduated from a foreign institution, one must have a credentialing agency vet the foreign degree. There are many such agencies, and they are competitive, prompt, and generally provide the required response.

- Once it is determined that the position requires a specific degree and that the noncitizen possesses that degree or equivalent, the next step in the application process is determining a prevailing wage. There are a number of fairly easy means of doing this, but regardless of the method chosen, the nonprofit employer must be able to attest to the U.S. Department of Labor that it is offering the noncitizen at least the prevailing wage. (In reality, the likelihood of having to defend the wage is small, because investigation only occurs if a complaint is lodged.)

- Finally, after the prevailing wage is determined, the employer files a Labor Condition Application (LCA) on Form ETA 9035 with the U.S. Department of Labor (DOL). The LCA is generally approved by return mail. The nonprofit then files the petition with CIS (Form I-129 with H supplement). On approval by CIS, the noncitizen applies at his or her home consulate for the visa — which is almost always a formality. The H-1 nonimmigrant may enter and leave the United States at will and may be paid any salary, so long as it is not less than what is shown on the LCA.

H-1B visas are granted for a maximum initial period of three years and may be renewed for an additional three years. And H-1B visas are employer-specific: If a noncitizen wishes to change H-1B employers, an entirely new petition must be filed with the CIS. However, once here as an H-1B, the noncitizen may begin work for a second employer as soon as the petition is filed — he or she need not wait for the approval. (Changing employers does not extend the six-year maximum period.)

The spouse and minor children of H-1B beneficiaries are accorded H-4 status and may enter and leave the United States at will, with or without the H-1B noncitizen. H-4 nonimmigrants are not allowed to work in the United States. But, if they choose, they may seek their own H-1 (or other) nonimmigrant status.

A response to an H-1B application is generally received from the CIS within four months. "Premium Processing," with an extra fee of $1,000, reduces the wait to two weeks or less.

EXCHANGE VISITORS, J STATUS

This category is for noncitizens, such as students, scholars, medical residents, business trainees, or camp counselors, seeking experience or coming to conduct research in the United States. But each J status application must be through a program established by an institutional sponsor, such as a think tank, medical school, international chamber of commerce, or other such organization, which has received approval of its program from the U.S. Department of State. (An employer may establish its own program — a fairly tedious process — or may, in effect, purchase participation in an established program, such as the Association for International Practical Training.)

The sponsor's program, once preapproved by the Department of State, is permitted to issue a Certificate of Eligibility (Form DS-2019) to qualified noncitizens. The noncitizen presents the approved form at the consulate and is granted a visa for the duration of the program. Students, scholars, and trainees each have specified maximum stays (for example, business trainees are limited to 18 months and medical residents to seven years).

Once in the United States, the J status noncitizen's employment is limited to the program sponsor. The spouse and minor children of the J noncitizen are accorded the same period of stay and may accept employment with government approval. Many J visa holders are saddled with a two-year home country preserve *requirement* at the ambassador of the program.

EXTRAORDINARY NONCITIZENS, O STATUS

This category covers those persons with "extraordinary" ability in the sciences, education, business, or athletics. Extraordinariness is established by receipt of a major recognized award, such as a Nobel prize, or stellar achievement, such as membership on an Olympic team. If this is not applicable, proof of at least three of the following considerations may qualify the applicant for this category:

- Receipt of other nationally or internationally recognized prizes related to the noncitizen's field of endeavor;

- Membership in associations that require peer review prior to acceptance;

- Publication of a textbook or chapter within a textbook or other internationally recognized publication;

- Service as a judge of the work of others in the field at issue;

- Proof of scholarly, scientific, or artistic contributions;

- Documentation of articles in peer reviewed publications;

- Display of artistic work at exhibitions in more than one country;

- Performance in a lead starring or critical role in an artistic organization with an established reputation;

- Evidence of a high salary;

- Evidence of commercial success in the performing arts;

- Other evidence showing extraordinary ability or achievement.

Additional, separate criteria control the admission of noncitizens in the arts, such as Oscar winners. The noncitizen artist must be coming to perform defined work or specified events; freelancing is not permitted. Three years is the maximum duration of stay, but extensions in one-year increments are possible.

The petition is filed with the CIS: I-129 with O supplement. Once approved, the noncitizen must apply to the U.S. Consulate in his or her country of residence.

RELIGIOUS WORKERS, R STATUS

Persons coming to the United States to perform truly religious functions, and not simply working for a religious organization as, for example, a nurse or executive, may be accorded R status. The CIS is relatively strict in its determination of what is a religious activity.

IMMIGRANT STATUS

The other major immigration category covers persons intending to reside in the United States indefinitely, referred to as lawful permanent residents (LPRs) or, in the vernacular, "green card" holders. Once a person attains LPR status, he or she has most of the rights and responsibilities of a citizen, with the singular exception of the right to vote. After one has been a permanent resident for five years (three years if the permanent residency was gained through marriage to a U.S. citizen), the LPR may petition for citizenship, a process known as naturalization.

As noted above, pursuing LPR status for a noncitizen is usually more lengthy and complicated than obtaining a nonimmigrant visa, but the latter can be obtained first while the longer LPR process is pursued.

There are two primary means of attaining LPR status: 1) by way of U.S. citizen or permanent resident relatives; or 2) by way of employment. Each of the two categories has "preferences" within it, which determine the noncitizen's place in line for permanent residence.

LPR STATUS THROUGH FAMILY RELATIONSHIP

Employers should always first investigate the possibility of permanent residence being achieved through a family relationship, because the process is generally less involved and less costly (though often slower). Employers should inquire of all prospective noncitizen hires whether they have relatives who are U.S. citizens, in order to ascertain whether that route should be pursued. However, immediate LPR status is only available to spouses of citizens and to parents of U.S. citizens of more than 21 years of age. The waiting time for children and siblings of U.S. citizens is substantial.

One potential disadvantage of an employee seeking permanent residence through a family relationship is that the employee is not tied to the employer in order to continue and complete of the process. Provided that nonimmigrant status is maintained, the family-related permanent residence process proceeds independently of the noncitizen's employment.

LPR STATUS THROUGH EMPLOYMENT

Immigration law establishes a number of "employment-based preferences" for LPR status. In general, the preference categories relate to the level of education attained by the applicant: the greater the educational level, the higher the preference. In turn, the higher the preference, the shorter the period one may be required to wait for an immigrant visa.

The First, Second, and Third Employment-Based Preferences are most likely of interest to nonprofit employers.

First Preference Petitions

First Preference noncitizens are those people at the very pinnacle of their profession (such as, Ph.Ds with published works or holders of internationally recognized awards). Persons in this category are generally at least in their 40s, command a six-figure salary, and are otherwise truly extraordinary. The most important part of a

First Preference petition is establishing the "extraordinary ability" of the noncitizen. As with the O nonimmigrant visa to which this is comparable, if the noncitizen is not a recipient of a Nobel Prize or other internationally recognized award, one must establish, through documentation, that the noncitizen satisfies at least three of the requirements to establish extraordinariness (see bottom of previous page).

Obviously, at this level of achievement, each noncitizen is unique and there is some room for originality in establishing that the person has reached the very top of his or her field. It is important to show the CIS why the noncitizen at issue is more than just very competent; the application must establish that the noncitizen has truly reached the top of his or her profession or avocation and has been recognized as a member of an elite club, as it were.

A second category of First Preference noncitizens are outstanding professors and researchers. In order to be included in this group, the professor or researcher must demonstrate recognition as an outstanding member of a specific academic field, at least three years of teaching or research in the field, and have an offer of a research or tenured teaching position, which typically is permanent in nature, or a comparable research position with a private employer that is also permanent. In order to satisfy this last qualification, the private employer must have at least three full-time researchers already and these other researchers must also have documented accomplishments in the field at issue. In order to demonstrate that the researcher or teacher is outstanding in his or her field, the rules require that at least two of the following be documented:

- Receipt of a major international prize or its equivalent;

- Membership in a peer reviewed association;

- Published material in a textbook or similar publication;

- Proof that the noncitizen has participated in the judging of others in the field of endeavor;

- Evidence of the scientific or scholarly research accomplished by the noncitizen;

- Authorship of articles in peer reviewed publications of international acclaim.

Second Preference Petitions

This category is generally utilized by persons with a master's or more advanced degree, who do not qualify for "extraordinary" status. As with the First Preference, there are several subcategories in the Second Preference classification. In order to establish "exceptional ability" (a lesser standard than the First Preference's "extraordinary ability"), the athlete, artist, researcher, or business person needs to document at least three of the following:

- A degree or diploma in the field at issue;

- Letters from current or former employers demonstrating 10 years of full-time experience in the occupation at issue;

- A license of certification relevant to the position at issue;

- High salary demonstrating exceptional ability;

- Membership in peer reviewed professional associations;

- Recognition for achievements and contributions to the industry; artistic field; or sport by peers, governmental entities, or professional and business associations.

A subcategory in the Second Preference that is often of use to nonprofits is "advanced degree professionals." Advanced degrees are defined as master's or above, or a bachelor's degree and at least five years of progressive experience in the specialty at issue. (The qualifying experience must have been gained after the noncitizen attained his or her bachelor's degree.) The petitioner will need to document the experience, explain how the experience is progressive in nature, and why the experience is required in order to perform adequately the job at issue. When a license is typically required in order to perform the job (such as a lawyer), the petitioner must demonstrate that the beneficiary has passed or is in the process of taking the qualifying exam. Even more detailed rules apply to health care professionals such as nurses, physicians, occupational therapists, and physical therapists.

Third Preference Petitions

This category includes professionals with at least a bachelor's degree, skilled workers performing a task that requires at least two years' of training and experience, and "other workers" who have less than two years of experience, to a maximum of 10,000 petitions a year. (In most prior years "other workers" have faced a very long backlog. The Third Preference has recently become backlogged for China, India, and the Phillipines.)

Labor Certification

The primary hurdle of Second and Third Preference petitions is the requirement for *Labor Certification*. An approved Labor Certification application is required in order to submit a Second Preference or Third Preference petition to CIS. The labor certification process is not handled by the CIS, but under the Department of Labor. The DOL certification is performed by the State Employment Service Agency (SESA), a federally funded and generally undermanned state bureaucracy that is frequently far behind in processing applications.

The purpose of a Labor Certification is not to find the best worker for a nonprofit job, but to determine whether any minimally qualified U.S. citizens are willing to take the job at issue. The fact that a noncitizen may have qualifications head and shoulders above any of the U.S. applicants is irrelevant. Also irrelevant are 1) the fact that the employer may have no intention of hiring any person other than the non-citizen; and 2) the employer's recruiting practices, unless they happen to fit within the precisely described recruitment procedures set forth by the Department of Labor. As the process is begun, the employer is under no obligation to hire anyone, including the noncitizen, and the fact that the noncitizen may be employed with the employer (typically pursuant to an H-1 visa) is also irrelevant; the current employment of the noncitizen does not affect the labor certification process one way or the other, except that employment with the petitioner cannot count toward the minimum experience required.

There are waivers, exemptions, and shortcuts available to speed up the Labor Certification process. But because the process is arcane and complex — and because of DOL understaffing and delays — professional counsel to navigate through the process should be sought by any prospective employee or nonprofit wishing to hire a noncitizen.

MAKING THE APPLICATION

Once the LPR preference application is approved, it can be processed either through the CIS or the Department of State's consular service. *Consular processing* occurs when one obtains an interview with the U.S. Consul in the applicant's country of residence. This process often proceeds more quickly (perhaps six to nine months from the date a petition is approved), as opposed to the year or two waiting period an applicant may have for a CIS "Adjustment of Status" interview in the United States. On the other hand, many noncitizens have no interest in returning to their home country and would prefer to wait out the process here.

CIS ADJUSTMENT OF STATUS (WHILE REMAINING IN THE UNITED STATES)

An applicant may file for Adjustment of Status (on Form I-485) at the same time as he or she files for an immigrant preference. While the adjustment of status application will not be adjudicated until the preference petition is approved, there are certain advantages to filing an early adjustment-of-status application. Once the I-485 application is filed, the noncitizen's spouse may apply immediately for work authorization. In many instances this is a very important benefit to the couple involved, in that the spouse may not have prior work authorization. The employment authorization will be adjudicated premised upon the adjustment-of-status *application*, as opposed to the adjustment-of-status *approval*.

Because adjustment of status is considered a special privilege, certain noncitizens are not accorded this benefit. First, noncitizens who did not enter the country legally initially may not adjust status because they have no status to begin with. The most important disqualification is that anyone who worked in the United States without authorization for more than six months, is barred from adjustment of status (unless the adjustment is based upon an immediate relative). Thus, before proceeding down the adjustment of status road, one must be sure that the noncitizen has always maintained his or her status in the United States, and that there has never been any substantial unauthorized employment.

In addition to those hurdles, the adjustment applicant must establish that he or she is otherwise admissible, in terms of good health, mental illness, lack of criminal convictions, and the like. Such factors, which often do not relate to nonimmigrant status, can determine whether adjustment is a possibility.

CONSULAR PROCESSING

If the noncitizen has no problem with returning to his or her own country (and many business noncitizens travel frequently to their home country anyway), consular processing is often a quicker route to follow. In this case, once the petition is approved, it is only necessary to indicate to the CIS that the consular processing route is to be followed. The paperwork is then transferred to the National Visa Center, which will send out detailed instructions as to what forms and documentation need to be provided. This will include, among other things, a "Police

Certificate" from every country where the noncitizen has lived more than six months since the age of 16. Obtaining this information can be a problem in many countries where such reports are not practically available. The Department of State provides a list of countries where such certificates are truly not available.

The consular process should be initiated immediately upon receiving approval of a preference petition, by assembling birth, marriage, and divorce certificates; Police Certificates; military records; and tax records, so that a response may be made promptly to the National Visa Center when its request is received. Again, the same rules of exclusion apply (health, criminal convictions, membership in certain organizations, and the like) — which in actual practice rarely arise. In addition, persons previously deported or "removed" from the United States, or those who entered without inspection, or otherwise have violated immigration procedures may have difficulty. The instructions (both in adjustment and consular processing) received from the relevant federal agency are quite detailed and precise, and it is essential that they be followed to the letter.

CHAPTER Q&As

Q: Can a foreign citizen serve on our nonprofit organization's board of directors?

A: Yes. There is no provision in federal or state law that prohibits a nonprofit organization from electing or appointing an individual to serve on its board of directors based on his or her national origin or citizenship. Accordingly, it will be necessary only to determine whether the individual is qualified to serve as a director under the provisions of the organization's bylaws. If, however, the foreign citizen was not a proper resident of the United States and was present in violation of immigration law, then as a matter of public policy and fiduciary duty, it would likely be inappropriate for the individual to continue to serve on the board.

Q: What is an H-1B visa?

A: A visa is a governmental permission for a foreign citizen to live and/or work in the United States. Possibly the most useful category to many nonprofits is the H-1B "specialized knowledge" status. In order to qualify for such a visa, the noncitizen must have a four-year college degree and be coming to the United States to fill the position requiring the specialized knowledge reflected in the decree.

As nonprofit organizations participate in a more global environment, immigration law concerns will become more pressing. Educational and health care organizations in particular will need to stay abreast of developments in this area of the law so that they can take maximum advantage of opportunities to secure visas for desired employees and volunteers. Particularly after 9/11, security concerns are more prevalent and even nonprofit organizations are expected to exercise due diligence regarding the immigration status of all of their employees and volunteers. Employment policies for the organization should be fair and consistently applied. The chief executive should work with counsel to determine which visa programs provide opportunities for the organization in its personnel recruitment efforts. Timing can be an essential ingredient in successful navigation of the immigration laws; for example no H-visas (except to certain educational and research institutions) are available until October 1, 2005. Accordingly, the chief executive will need to pay close attention to the calendar in ongoing planning for the organization.

QUESTIONS THE BOARD SHOULD ASK

- Is our organization welcoming ethnic and cultural diversity?

- Do we monitor the demographics of our constituents and customers?

- Do we regularly verify the legal status of our new employees?

9.
Antitrust Law

E. John Steren

Antitrust laws are not solely the concern of Fortune 500 companies. Increasingly, they are also being applied to nonprofit organizations that act more like commercial enterprises, engaging in combinations, affiliations, mergers, and joint ventures that raise antitrust issues.

Nonprofit organizations are sometimes perceived as competing unfairly with their for-profit counterparts. However, the antitrust laws for the most part apply to nonprofits as well, and the government has in many instances been very aggressive in pursuing antitrust violations by nonprofits. This has particularly been the case in the field of health care. There is also another area of the law that helps to ensure a level playing field between nonprofits and for-profits. Under federal tax law, most tax-exempt organizations that carry on activities that are commercial in nature and not directly related to their exempt purposes must pay tax on the income generated from these activities, even though the organization is otherwise tax exempt. Thus, from a tax standpoint, they are treated the same as commercial enterprises when they operate in a commercial fashion.

Federal and state antitrust laws aim to protect consumers from the adverse effects and inefficient consequences (such as higher prices, lower-quality goods, and reduction in output) that can be the result of anticompetitive behavior. Those laws strive to achieve this objective by maintaining the integrity of an open and competitive market system that, in turn, promotes the efficient allocation of our economy's resources.

Importantly, the antitrust laws protect competition, not individual competitors. Inefficient firms that are unable to survive in a competitive environment lack recourse under the antitrust laws. In fact, the only time the antitrust laws seek to protect an individual competitor is when the elimination of that competitor adversely impacts competition in the market, ultimately causing harm to consumers.

APPLICATION OF THE ANTITRUST LAWS TO NONPROFITS

Contrary to popular misconception, there is no blanket exemption for nonprofits from antitrust laws. Nonprofits are specifically exempted from only one federal antitrust law, the Robinson-Patman Act, which prohibits a manufacturer from discriminating in price between buyers when such discrimination has an adverse effect on competition.

A few courts have held that the antitrust laws do not apply to the noncommercial activities of nonprofits. In other words, those courts have recognized that, as long as the potentially anticompetitive activities of a nonprofit are within the scope of its exempt nonprofit mission, then it will be exempt from antitrust laws. Nonprofits, particularly in the health care industry, have increasingly tried to play the "nonprofit card" to justify (or rationalize) anticompetitive behavior. For example, nonprofit participants in a potentially unlawful merger frequently point out in defense of their transaction that they have no shareholders, that their boards consist of community representatives, and that they lack the profit-maximizing incentives of for-profit entities. Therefore, even if they were to obtain market power (that is, the power to increase prices) as the result of their merger, such power would not be used.

This argument, however, ignores the fact that all board members owe a fiduciary duty to the nonprofit entities they serve, and that, although such entities may not have a profit-maximizing incentive, anticompetitive behavior engaged in by nonprofit entities still adversely affects the efficient allocation of resources and ultimately harms consumers. Most courts, therefore, discount or rule out completely a "nonprofit defense" to anticompetitive behavior.

What Conduct Is Prohibited by Antitrust Statutes?

The Sherman Act

The Sherman Act is the anchor of federal antitrust laws. The Act prohibits two kinds of behavior:

1. any contract, combination, or conspiracy among two or more parties that unreasonably restrains trade or commerce (Section 1 of the Act), and

2. unilateral conduct by one party that has an adverse effect upon competition, such as monopolizing, or attempting to monopolize, trade or commerce (Section 2).

An important point regarding Section 1 is that the terms *contract*, *combination*, and *conspiracy* are read broadly to encompass all types of concerted behavior. Agreements need not be explicit or written, but can often be inferred from circumstantial evidence relating to the conduct of the parties involved. All that is required is a "meeting of minds in an unlawful agreement." Unlawful agreements can be tacit, can arise without verbal communications, and can even be the result of coercion.

To violate Section 1, the agreement must involve parties that are legally capable of conspiring. The courts have determined that certain parties share such a closely aligned economic interest that, for purposes of the antitrust laws, they are legally incapable of conspiring. For example, a nonprofit and its wholly owned subsidiary are legally incapable of reaching an agreement between them that would violate Section 1. And a corporation generally cannot conspire with its employees nor can two sister corporations that share a common parent reach an agreement that violates Section 1.

Section 2 of the Sherman Act generally seeks to curb abuses by a single entity that result from the use of its *monopoly power*. Monopoly power (essentially nothing more than a heightened degree of market power) is defined as the ability to control prices or exclude competition. One indicator of monopoly power is an organization's market share. Generally speaking, an organization with a greater than 70 percent market share is presumed to have monopoly power, while an organization with less than 50 percent market share is not likely to have monopoly power. Organizations with market shares between 50 percent and 70 percent fall within a grey area.

Being a monopoly is not, in and of itself, unlawful. A claim of unlawful monopolization must contain two elements: 1) the possession of monopoly power in the relevant market; and 2) the willful acquisition or maintenance of that power. Companies that achieve monopoly status by virtue of natural growth through superior product, business acumen, or even by regulation are perfectly lawful. On the other hand, companies that attempt to achieve or maintain their monopoly status through the use of conduct that serves no purpose but to adversely affect competitors have acted improperly.

A claim of attempted monopolization — as opposed to one of existing monopoly — contains three elements: 1) conduct on the part of the defendant that is "predatory" or anticompetitive; 2) a specific intent by the defendant to monopolize; and 3) a dangerous probability that, if the conduct continues, the defendant will achieve monopoly power.

To prove either a monopolization or an attempted-monopolization claim, the plaintiff must show that the defendant engaged in predatory or anticompetitive conduct. There is often a fine line between conduct characterized as aggressive competition and conduct that is predatory. Conduct is labeled predatory only if it lacks a rational business justification other than to exclude actual or potential competitors from the market. Pricing products at below their cost, pressuring distributors to carry only the defendant's brand, and sometimes even the use of discounts designed to ensure customer loyalty are types of conduct that have been labeled as predatory.

A defendant's market share again plays a significant role in a claim of attempted monopolization and is the primary factor in determining whether a defendant is likely to succeed in obtaining monopoly power. Although there are no exact lines, a market share in excess of 50 percent is usually sufficient to satisfy this element while a market share below 30 percent is generally not sufficient. It is market shares between 30 percent and 50 percent that present a very nebulous area.

THE CLAYTON ACT

The Clayton Act, enacted subsequent to the Sherman Act, attempts to prohibit other actions not specifically addressed by the Sherman Act, but which also have a potential adverse effect on competition. The most significant provision of the Clayton Act prohibits any merger or acquisition (including stock and asset acquisition, mergers, and joint ventures) that may substantially lessen competition or tend to create a monopoly. And, unlike other antitrust laws, the Clayton Act seeks to predict and then prevent potentially unlawful conduct, rather than rectifying unlawful conduct already occurring.

The federal enforcement agencies take the following five-step approach to analyzing the likely anticompetitive effects of a proposed transaction: 1) define the relevant market and determine the level of concentration in the market, as well as the likely change in concentration level as a result of the transaction; 2) determine whether the change in concentration presents any competitive concerns; 3) determine the likelihood of a new entry or expansion in the market that might counteract the competitive concerns raised by the transaction; 4) consider possible efficiencies generated by the transaction as a procompetitive benefit that might otherwise not be achieved in the absence of the transaction; and 5) determine, if applicable, whether the transaction would prevent the exit of a failing firm from the market.

The Clayton Act requires all parties to a transaction that meet certain thresholds to report that transaction to both the Department of Justice and the Federal Trade Commission and to delay consummation of the transaction until the enforcement agencies have had an opportunity to investigate the potential anticompetitive consequences of the proposed transaction. All transactions valued in excess of $200 million are reportable. Also, acquisitions valued in excess of $50 million but less than $200 million are reportable if one party to the transaction has at least $10 million in annual sales or assets, and the other party has at least $100 million in annual sales or assets.

THE ROBINSON-PATMAN ACT

The Robinson-Patman Act seeks to establish a level playing field by prohibiting a manufacturer from discriminating in price between buyers when such discrimination has an adverse effect on competition. Although the scope of this statute covers all types of buyers, it was enacted with the intention of enabling smaller retailers to compete against larger chain stores that have historically benefited from their superior buying power.

This Act generally prohibits a manufacturer from selling the same or similar commodities to competing retailers at different prices. Also prohibited is the discrimination in the provision of marketing allowances and the payment of unjustified brokerage fees that serve as nothing more than bribes. The Robinson-Patman Act also imposes liability upon a buyer that knowingly receives or induces a discriminatory price.

There are certain exceptions to the Act's prohibition on price discrimination. A manufacturer is permitted to charge different prices when it is 1) attempting in good faith to meet a competitor's price; or 2) when the differential is directly related to a difference in cost associated with the manufacturing, packaging, or shipping of the item. Also, a manufacturer can offer discounts (including volume discounts) on its goods as long as such discounts are available, as a practical not just theoretical matter, to all buyers.

As mentioned above, the only exemption from antitrust laws that is unique to nonprofit entities is provided in the Robinson-Patman Act. Specifically, nonprofits are exempted from the Act's antidiscrimination provisions when nonprofits purchase items for their "own use."

What constitutes an entity's "own use" is, of course, the central question. In general, if the resale is to a person or entity that is a part of and promotes the intended purpose and operation of the nonprofit, then it is likely to satisfy the definition of "own use." For example, the resale of pharmaceutical products by a nonprofit hospital to its employees, retirees, volunteers, medical staff (for their own use or that of their dependents), and contract workers have all satisfied the "own use" exemption. Also, resale by a nonprofit hospital to its wholly owned clinics for use by those clinics in the treatment of their patients has been found to satisfy the "own use" definition. Similarly, the sale of bowling equipment to a university for use by the university students was held to be exempt.

In addition, transfers at cost between nonaffiliated nonprofit entities are also exempt. Although this transfer would not satisfy the "own use" definition, the receiving entity can take advantage of its own exemption, and — as long as the selling entity is not making a profit — the resale is not subject to the Robinson-Patman Act.

ANALYZING NONPROFIT CONDUCT UNDER FEDERAL ANTITRUST LAWS

Let's assume a nonprofit is considering a merger, acquisition, or joint venture that may give it a dominating role in the marketplace for the services it offers. How can the nonprofit determine whether it will run afoul of the antitrust laws?

Over time, the courts have developed three methods for analyzing conduct under the antitrust laws.

"PER SE" METHOD

Simplistic and egregious conduct is "*per se*" unlawful under the antitrust laws. This is conduct that will, without fail, create unjustified anticompetitive effects and lack any redeeming procompetitive benefits. As a result, no market analysis is required and no procompetitive benefits will be considered in defense of this conduct. (And per se conduct is more at risk for criminal prosecution.) The following are examples of agreements that constitute per se antitrust violations:

- *Price Fixing Agreements*

  A naked agreement between competitors on the same level of the distribution chain (referred to as "horizontal" competitors) relating to the price they will charge for their product or service (regardless of the reasonableness of the price), is a per se violation of the antitrust laws. The per se rule applies not only to direct agreements as to price, but also to all sorts of agreements that affect the price. Agreements that raise, lower, peg, or stabilize prices, including agreements relating to credit, discounts, costs, markups, and surcharges, are all potential per se violations of the antitrust laws.

- *Market Allocation Agreements*

  Agreements between competitors as to the products or services they will or will not provide, the geographical areas they will or will not serve, and agreements relating to the division of customers or types of customers are all per se violations. Even a laudable rationale for the allocation, such as the creation of "centers of excellence," will not provide a defense for this conduct.

- *Refusal To Deal (Group Boycotts)*

  Refusals to deal (or group boycotts) refer to agreements between horizontal competitors not to deal, or only to deal with a third party on agreed-upon terms. These agreements constitute per se violations when the defendants possess market power.

- *Tying Arrangements*

  A tying arrangement occurs when one party agrees to sell one product or service to another party, but only on the condition that the buyer agrees to purchase a second product or service from the same seller, or agrees not to purchase the second product or service from another seller. The first product is referred to as the tying product, and the second item is the tied product. These arrangements are per se unlawful when the seller has market power in the tying product.

- *Bid Rigging*

  Agreements affecting the outcome of a competitive bidding process, including agreements relating to who will or will not bid and prices on competitive bids, are per se violations.

"RULE OF REASON" METHOD

While egregious conduct with no procompetitive justification is per se illegal, most conduct is not so clear-cut. Most types of conduct, such as agreements between joint-venture partners, can have both anticompetitive and procompetitive effects. The rule of reason is the method most frequently used to analyze those effects. This approach incorporates a detailed analysis of the relevant market and the likely effects of the conduct within that market, and seeks to balance the potential anticompetitive effects against the likely procompetitive benefits of the conduct.

The plaintiff or prosecutor has the initial burden of showing that the agreement has or is likely to have an adverse effect on competition. If met, the burden then shifts to the defendant to demonstrate that the conduct can or will achieve procompetitive benefits. The burden will then shift back to the plaintiff to show that the conduct at issue is not reasonably necessary to achieve the proffered benefits, that is, there are other less restrictive means of achieving the claimed efficiencies.

Analysis under the rule of reason usually requires as an initial step defining the relevant market affected by the conduct at issue. A relevant market includes both a relevant product market (the identification of the product or service, including all reasonable substitutes), and a relevant geographic market (the geographic area where the product or service is sold and where consumers can reasonably turn to find the relevant product or service).

Once the relevant market is defined, the inquiry moves to a determination of whether the defendant has market power (the ability to raise prices above the competitive level) in the relevant market. This is usually determined by looking first at the defendant's market share and then assessing other relevant market factors such as high barriers to entry to determine whether the defendant possesses market power. Generally speaking, the threshold market share required to show that a defendant possesses market power is 30 percent.

When the market power analysis is completed, the inquiry then focuses on whether the conduct at issue would adversely affect competition by creating, increasing, or protecting the defendant's market power, or facilitating its exercise. If the conduct does adversely affect competition, then, as previously stated, the burden shifts to the defendant to demonstrate the potential procompetitive justifications, including efficiencies generated by the agreement.

"Quick-Look Rule of Reason" Method

Somewhere between the rule of reason and the per se rule lies the quick-look rule of reason. This is a relatively recent approach to antitrust analysis that has been applied in situations involving agreements among competitors that create unreasonable restraints, but which might have counterbalancing and prevailing justifications. Under the approach, the court will make an initial inquiry into whether the proffered justifications for the conduct are plausible and whether the anticompetitive effects of the conduct are apparent. If the justifications are not plausible, and if the anticompetitive effects are apparent, then the conduct will be condemned. However, if the justifications are plausible, or if the adverse effects are not readily apparent, then the court will engage in a full rule-of-reason analysis.

Enforcement of the Antitrust Laws

The Antitrust Division of the Department of Justice (DOJ) and the Federal Trade Commission (FTC) are the federal agencies empowered to enforce the federal antitrust laws. DOJ is authorized to enforce all of the federal antitrust laws, with the exception of the Federal Trade Commission Act. DOJ can bring civil actions seeking both monetary and injunctive relief and, when appropriate, criminal actions against offenders of the federal antitrust laws.

The authority of the FTC is restricted to enforcement of the Federal Trade Commission Act, the Clayton Act, and the Robinson-Patman Act. Although it cannot directly enforce the Sherman Act, its enforcement authority under the FTC Act to police all unfair methods of competition and unfair or deceptive acts or practices is broad enough to cover conduct proscribed by the Sherman Act. The FTC can bring a claim for both monetary and injunctive relief, but has no criminal authority. If criminal action is warranted, the matter must be referred to DOJ.

The FTC has only limited authority to regulate the conduct of nonprofit entities. The FTC Act specifically limits the FTC's enforcement powers to entities that "carry on business for its own profit or that of its members." The FTC reads this broadly to permit it to have jurisdiction over any nonprofit entity that devotes a substantial part of its activities toward providing a pecuniary benefit to its members. As a result, while a merger between two nonprofit entities may not be subject to review by the FTC, a nonprofit association, such as a trade association, that engages in anticompetitive activities with or for the benefit of its for-profit members may find its activities scrutinized by the FTC.

Most states also have their own antitrust laws that generally mirror the federal law. In certain limited circumstances, states can bring actions under the federal antitrust statutes to recover damages on behalf of its citizens or when the state itself is injured by a violation of the antitrust laws.

Finally, private parties can bring claims for both monetary and injunctive relief under the Sherman, Clayton, and Robinson-Patman Acts. Successful litigants are entitled to triple damages and attorneys' fees. It should also be noted that the cost of defending such actions, even if frivolous, can be staggering.

CHAPTER Q&As

Q: Are nonprofits immune from the application of the antitrust laws?

A: Contrary to popular belief, there is no blanket exemption for nonprofits from the antitrust laws. Nonprofits are specifically exempted from only one federal antitrust law, the Robinson-Patman Act, which prohibits a manufacturer from discriminating in price between buyers when such discrimination has an adverse effect on competition. However, a few courts have held that the antitrust laws do not apply to the noncommercial activities of nonprofits.

Q: Who enforces the antitrust laws? Who can bring an antitrust claim?

A: The Antitrust Division of the Department of Justice and the Federal Trade Commission are the federal agencies empowered to enforce the federal antitrust laws. The Department of Justice can bring civil actions seeking both monetary and injunctive relief and, when appropriate, criminal actions against offenders of the federal antitrust laws. Most states also have their own antitrust laws that generally mirror the federal laws. Finally, private parties can bring claims for both monetary and injunctive relief under the Sherman, Clayton, and Robinson-Patman Acts.

The antitrust laws may not have direct impact for many nonprofit organizations in their day-to-day operations. However, board members and the chief executive should be diligent in staying abreast of developments in this area to avoid traps for the unwary. A key element of the antitrust laws is their enforcement, and some government administrations have been more active than others in this regard. Health care organizations are the most likely target for review of antitrust violations. Nonprofit organizations should seek the advice of counsel regarding the extent to which the antitrust laws may impact the ability of the organization's staff or governing body to meet with other organizations for planning or carrying on joint activities. Even when a particular nonprofit organization is not likely to receive antitrust scrutiny of its operations, the board should have a general understanding of these rules since they may affect the conduct of larger organizations with whom they have dealings.

QUESTIONS THE BOARD SHOULD ASK

- Do we have a clear policy and guidelines for assessing the fees for our products and services for various constituents?

- Do we retain a lawyer to review our contracts?

- Have we been apprised by counsel and management of the types of activities that lead to antitrust scrutiny in our field?

10.
Criminal Investigations

Martha P. Rogers and Leon Rodriguez

Federal and state government investigations have become a fact of life for nonprofit organizations, as they are subjected to an increasing number of statutes that impose criminal liability. Regardless of their underlying merit, such investigations and government scrutiny put considerable pressure on any nonprofit organization. Board and employee morale at all levels may suffer as the result of anxiety and uncertainty about the consequences of the investigation. Cash flow may be jeopardized as reserves are set aside to pay legal fees and possible fines and penalties. Vendors and donors may also lose confidence, as news of the investigation becomes widespread.

When a criminal investigation is underway, clearly such a development should be a top priority for the board of directors. Timing is critical, and the board and chief executive should not delay in consulting with experienced legal counsel. Special meetings of the executive committee or even the full board may be necessary to ensure that the board is properly informed and can provide meaningful and timely input. If the investigation involves allegations regarding the chief executive, the executive committee or board will need to meet in executive session with the organization's legal counsel to ensure that appropriate information is being provided to the board without being filtered through the chief executive. The board must be prepared to act promptly to protect the organization against any further potentially criminal activity. The organization should contact its D&O insurance carrier to advise them of any potential or actual criminal charges. The board must also be prepared to handle the public relations consequences of any public disclosure of the criminal investigation. Consultation with staff, legal counsel, and for larger organizations, a media relations consultant, would be warranted.

The inherent nature of investigations can push organizational stress beyond the point of tolerance because investigators disclose little about their activities, either to the subjects of an investigation or otherwise to the outside world. An organization under investigation learns about only a small portion of the investigative steps taken in its case. The law enforcement justifications for such secrecy are readily understandable. But from an organization's perspective, nothing fuels more fear than a dearth of knowledge about an investigation and the consequent appearance that the investigation is arbitrary and incoherent. Making matters worse, government investigations often continue for years before reaching a conclusion.

Nevertheless, most government inquiries into misconduct proceed according to a common template. (See Investigative Timeline on page 103.) An understanding of the elements common to white collar investigations can illuminate much of what happens when a nonprofit organization is the subject of an investigation. Those board members and executives who understand this template will be better able to help the organization's counsel address the investigation and to defend against any resulting charges.

MAKING A CASE

Essentially, a government investigation is a campaign to "make its case," that is, to gather and process sufficient evidence to support a criminal prosecution. Government prosecutors initiate an investigation after they receive information that substantially arouses their suspicion that a violation of the law has occurred. Such allegations can come from many sources: civilian witnesses, audit findings, disgruntled employees, or as a spin-off from another investigation.

Not surprisingly, while the judicial system may presume that defendants are innocent until proven guilty, the investigative process works from the contrary assumption. Although as a matter of ethics, investigators who come across facts helpful to the subject of an investigation must consider and weigh such evidence, nonprofits should understand that government investigators do not look for exculpatory evidence to the same degree as they do for incriminating evidence. This means that once the government begins to build a case, the subject of that investigation should immediately begin to address the issues raised by the investigation.

Anyone who comes into contact with a government investigation, either as a subject or a witness, is well-advised never to address the inquiry without the assistance of experienced counsel. In addition to providing advice about the course of the investigation and acting as a liaison with the government, counsel will initiate a defense investigation. The purpose of a defense investigation is to probe the assumptions underlying the government's case and to develop evidence that tends to exonerate the organization.

In the federal justice system, law enforcement agents from the Federal Bureau of Investigation, as well as a host of other federal, state, and local investigative agencies, conduct the fieldwork in an investigation. They receive legal advice from prosecutors and attorneys in one of the 94 U.S. Attorneys' Offices throughout the country or in specialized units based at the Department of Justice in Washington, D.C. The prosecutor makes the ultimate determination about whether to seek charges in a case and will prosecute the case in court if charges are brought. In criminal cases, the prosecutor utilizes a grand jury, an assembly of between 16–23 citizens empanelled to investigate alleged wrongdoing and to consider charges proposed by the prosecutor. (As a practical matter, grand juries agree to charges proposed by the prosecutor in 99.9 percent of all cases.)

INVESTIGATIVE TECHNIQUES AND PROCEDURES

The most basic work of the investigation is the search for proof that the alleged wrongdoing was motivated by guilty intent, rather than caused by honest error or mere negligence. It is the element of criminal intent — the intent to knowingly violate the law — that differentiates a civil from a criminal case. For this reason, fraud investigators devote considerable time looking for evidence of an organization's motive and intent at the time the actions under investigation occurred. In particular, investigators may seek out oral or written statements that the organization and its officers, directors, and staff have made that pertain to the alleged criminal activity, and also to examine documents, such as financial records, that may unveil an organization's motives.

Initially, most investigations are conducted in secret, in order to take certain steps that might not be possible if the organization were to know of the investigation. When the investigators substantially exhaust the covert portion of the investigation, they commence the more visible part. Investigations become overt either because organizations learn about them through leaks or, more typically, after the occurrence of an investigative step directed specifically at the organization. In both the covert and overt parts of an investigation, investigators may use the following techniques.

OBTAINING DOCUMENTARY EVIDENCE BY SUBPOENA

This includes gathering documents obtained either through voluntary disclosure by witnesses or through compelled production under a grand jury or other subpoena. Investigators will also search government and public records for documents, such as tax and other financial records of the nonprofit organization and its officers and board members, that may pertain to the investigation.

A *subpoena* is an order of a court (or a government agency) that requires an individual to testify or to produce documents, or both, on or before a certain date. There are many different types of subpoenas (state, federal, grand jury, administrative). If your organization is served with a subpoena, the following advice should be followed:

- Even if you think you or your organization has done nothing improper, receipt of a subpoena is a legal development that should be taken very seriously and should be addressed by experienced counsel. Do not attempt to respond to a subpoena without the assistance of an attorney. The subpoena may, for example, ask for documents to which the government is not entitled, such as attorney-client privileged documents. It is in the organization's best interest that all communications with the government concerning a subpoena be through an attorney experienced in subpoena compliance. In certain circumstances, even the act of producing documents may result in unwanted consequences.

- Unfortunately, subpoenas are often extremely broad. In many situations, government attorneys may be willing to negotiate with your counsel to narrow the terms of the subpoena or agree to a "rolling production" of evidence, by which documents are produced over a period of time as they are located, numbered, and copied.

- Some subpoenas appear to require the recipient of the subpoena to *create* documents in response to the subpoena. The government cannot generally require you to create documents to give to them, although this may be something you are willing to do as part of negotiating with government counsel on other requirements of the subpoena. Nevertheless, creating documents to comply with a subpoena should be carefully discussed with a nonprofit's counsel.

- Receipt of a subpoena is an obvious sign that an investigation is underway. It is possible, however, that the subject of the investigation is not your organization, but Company X or Individual Y, and that the government is only seeking documents from your organization to learn something about your organization's relationship with Company X or Individual Y. Nonetheless, be aware that, depending on what is revealed by the documents turned over to it, the government could decide to turn its focus on your organization.

- Investigative agents will, in most cases, personally serve a subpoena on the custodian of records at an organization and, while doing so, may attempt to interview one or more of the employees on site. The nonprofit's management should make all employees aware immediately that they are under no obligation to be interviewed and have the right to have an attorney present if they do decide to be interviewed. Even if no attempt is made to interview employees when the subpoena is served, it is possible that the government will attempt to contact employees at home to interview them without their employer's knowledge. Employees should be advised that government agents may attempt to contact them at home and should be advised of their rights and responsibilities in the event this happens.

- Be sure to identify for the nonprofit's attorneys all relevant documents — even if you think the documents will hurt the organization's case. Counsel must be aware of all documents so they can be evaluated before being produced to the government.

- Immediately upon receipt of a subpoena, all employees should be instructed not to destroy or alter in any way any documents or e-mails. While some organizations have document retention and destruction policies in place as a normal practice, these policies may allow for the destruction of certain documents that the government is seeking through its subpoena. Therefore, standard document retention and destruction policies should be immediately suspended once a subpoena is served on the organization.

OBTAINING DOCUMENTARY EVIDENCE BY SEARCH WARRANT

Generally, subpoenas, rather than search warrants, are employed for larger, established organizations. But a search warrant may be utilized instead of or as well as a subpoena. A *search warrant* is a court order obtained by prosecutors that gives law enforcement agents the right to enter the premises identified in the warrant for the purpose of seizing any documents and objects specified in the warrant. In order to obtain approval for a search warrant, the government must establish before a judge or agency that there is probable cause to believe that the premises to be searched will contain evidence of a specified criminal activity.

The government's primary purpose in executing a search warrant is to surprise the organization, with the hopes of obtaining information the government believes it would be unable to obtain otherwise — for example, by a subpoena. If, in the unfortunate case your nonprofit is served with a search warrant, what are the right — and wrong — things to do?

- Ask the agent in charge of the search to identify himself or herself and the agency. Do not volunteer any information about your organization or its employees.

- The execution of a search warrant means that the government believes that a crime has occurred. It is imperative that a nonprofit served with a warrant obtain competent and experienced counsel. Immediately contact your organization's legal department to inform them that agents have arrived with a search warrant. If no one in the department is available or if your organization has no legal department, call the attorneys who usually handle your organization's legal work.

- Ask the government agents to postpone their search until your attorneys can be present. Although they are not required to observe your request — and probably won't agree to it — if by chance they do agree, it will be better to wait for your counsel.

- If the agents refuse to wait until your attorney's arrival, review the search warrant to determine where it allows them to search and what types of documents it allows them to seize. Also ask for the affidavit in support of the search warrant, which had to be presented to the court to demonstrate that the agents have probable cause to believe that the premises contain evidence of a specified criminal activity. Even though the affidavit is often sealed, and thus is probably not immediately available, it nevertheless should be asked for.

- If the agents ask for consent to search areas other than those authorized by the search warrant or to take documents other than those specified in the search warrant, tell them that you want to wait until an attorney is present to advise you as to whether you should consent to their request. Do not consent to a search for records that are not specified in the search warrant or for locations not specified in the warrant (for example, offsite storage) without speaking to your lawyer.

- Sometimes when serving a subpoena and almost always when executing a search warrant, investigators will attempt to interview a nonprofit's employees. A search warrant does not give agents the right to conduct such interviews, so you should send employees home immediately to remove them from that possibility. Employees who remain should be advised that they do not have to consent to be interviewed (it is the decision of each employee whether or not to be interviewed). The organization should provide an attorney to be present during any such interview, if the employee agrees to be interviewed and would like counsel to be present.

- If agents attempt to seize or examine privileged communications between your organization and its attorneys, you should request they wait to do so until your attorney has arrived so that your attorney can discuss the matter with them.

- You are not required to assist the agents in any way during their search. This means that you do not have to tell them where the documents that they want are located, nor do you have any obligation to answer questions about the content or meaning of the documents they are examining and seizing.

- After the premises have been searched, the agents are required to leave an inventory of the items they have seized, though on most occasions it is written in such a way as to be useless (for example, "box of financial records"). Try to obtain — or create for yourself — a detailed list of the documents seized.

WITNESS INTERVIEWS AND CONSENSUAL RECORDING

In the covert phase of an investigation, agent interviews or grand jury questioning of witnesses — who are not expected to disclose the existence of the investigation to the subjects of it — will probably occur. Where useful and feasible, cooperating witnesses may also be asked by investigators to engage in surreptitiously recorded conversations with subjects concerning the matters under investigation.

Once the organization becomes aware of an investigation or agents have gone as far as they can with covert operations, the investigation enters an overt phase and the investigators cast a wider net in order to complete their investigation. They interview more witnesses, and a number of witnesses may receive subpoenas directing them to appear and testify before the grand jury. Throughout this process, the investigative team reviews documents and interview reports in an effort to uncover evidence that will help build a prosecution case and to isolate additional leads to other evidence useful to the prosecution.

Covert investigative activity, however, may continue even after an organization knows of the existence of an investigation. For example, investigators might stage encounters between cooperating witnesses and employees, officers, or directors of the organization during the time following the service of a subpoena or the execution of a search warrant, since those events provide an excellent opportunity for incriminating conversations.

STAYING THE COURSE DURING AN INVESTIGATION

Although some investigations conclude quickly, most take years before the prosecutor makes a decision whether or not to prosecute. The merit of a case is not necessarily directly proportional to the duration of the investigation. Rather, the length of the inquiry depends on the amount of investigative work necessary to reach a decision and on the priority given to the case by the prosecutor. Often, cases without merit drag on unnecessarily as prosecutors direct their attention to higher-priority cases. However, one factor decisively limits the length of an investigation: All federal criminal statutes are subject to statutes of limitation. For most white collar or fraud crimes, statutes of limitation require prosecution to be initiated no later than five years from the date of an alleged criminal act, or, in the case of criminal tax offenses, within six years.

If an investigation drags on for months and then years, a nonprofit board and staff may become understandably frustrated. A natural temptation during this period is for an organization's board or executives to become impatient to tell the government their side of the story. After all, what could better bring an investigation to a favorable conclusion than for the prosecutor to hear what happened from those most directly involved? With very rare exceptions, defense attorneys will advise their clients against such impetuous soul baring. By offering one's side of the case, an organization may relinquish important protections such as the privilege against self-incrimination and the privilege that safeguards communications between clients and attorneys. But the greatest risk is that the government may garner evidence that seems harmless enough to the organization, and possibly even its lawyer, but which in fact is an important piece of the puzzle for the prosecutor, or paves the way for prosecution of offenses related to false statements to the government.

During this waiting period, there will be meetings between the organization's attorneys and the prosecutor. The prosecutor may meet with a nonprofit's attorneys in an effort to settle the case in advance of filing in court. Alternatively, defense attorneys may request such a meeting in an effort to persuade the prosecution that its case is not viable.

The investigative process ultimately culminates in a prosecutorial decision. In most cases, the prosecutor will first decide whether to proceed criminally. Usually a decision to bring criminal charges is reviewed at several supervisory levels within the prosecutor's office. Not infrequently during the course of such review, supervisors return cases for more investigation in order to resolve questions they have identified during their internal review. During this time, defense counsel often avail themselves of the opportunity to try to convince the prosecutor's supervisor of the case's lack of merit. This is infrequently successful, but usually worth the effort.

If the prosecutors decide not to bring any charges, they do not necessarily notify an organization of this fact. But their silence is golden and should not be disturbed. There is an understandable urge by directors and executives of a nonprofit under investigation to seek a final resolution. Yet there is considerable risk in inquiring whether a prosecutor has declined a case: A case that had been dormant and ignored may roar back to life after a prosecutor or his or her supervisor has reviewed the file. The following chart illustrates an example of an investigative timeline.

INVESTIGATIVE TIMELINE

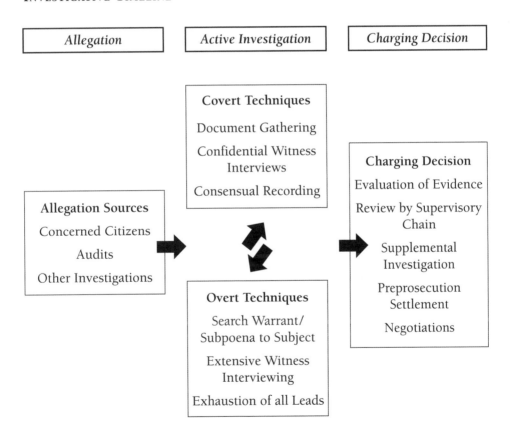

Nonprofit organizations, despite their noble purposes, do run afoul of the criminal law. Newspapers all too often run stories of embezzlement by employees entrusted with stewardship of charitable assets. Chief executives sometimes treat their nonprofit as a source of personal funds. Directors may funnel the organization's revenues into companies in which they have a financial interest through sweetheart deals. The organization's employees may violate laws intended to protect federal programs from fraud and abuse. When these types of abuse occur, federal and state prosecutors often launch investigations to determine who is responsible and to probe for broader patterns of criminal activity. When the chief executive or the board receives information indicating that an investigation may be underway, prompt consultation with legal counsel experienced in criminal law matters is critical. The chief executive should understand the impact of receiving a subpoena, search warrant, or other inquiry from law enforcement officials and should be knowledgeable and confident of the organization's rights when this occurs.

QUESTIONS THE BOARD SHOULD ASK

- Do we have policies addressing whistleblowers and document destruction?

- Do we have a solid policy on disaster and crisis management?

- Do our internal controls provide adequate protection against potential misconduct and negligence by board members or staff?

11.
Litigation and Alternative Dispute Resolution

Jeffrey A. Regner

Legal disputes can arise from a variety of sources: other nonprofits; employees, clients, or vendors; for-profit competitors; and the government. Some may be easily resolved by a simple phone call or meeting, while others require more involved methods of resolution.

The most well-known means of addressing disputes in civil society is the lawsuit — or litigation. But, increasingly, disputing parties are turning to means other than lawsuits to resolve disagreements. These other methods, such as arbitration and mediation, are commonly referred to as *alternative dispute resolution* or ADR.

When a dispute arises involving a nonprofit, it is important to make a meaningful analysis to determine the most appropriate and advantageous means of resolving it. In many instances, more than one method may be usefully employed. For example, nonbinding mediation often will precede arbitration or a court trial. In other situations, a minitrial on hotly disputed issues may be followed by mediation of larger issues. In some instances, a single dispute may be broken down into logical parts for separate resolution of each issue.

One often overlooked aspect of resolving a dispute is the public relations implications for a nonprofit, especially when the organization is involved in a high-profile case. Criminal charges against a nonprofit's directors or senior executives — a worst-case example — can set off an avalanche of unfavorable publicity. Even a simple lawsuit by a former employee for wrongful discharge can erupt into negative media coverage for a nonprofit — as, for example, this headline: "Homeless Organization's Laid-Off Employee Now Homeless." Any nonprofit involved in significant litigation or other dispute resolution should make public perception a consideration in all its strategic decisions about the case, consulting, if possible, public relations professionals as well as legal counsel.

In addition, boards should anticipate that employee morale may suffer as a result of anxiety and uncertainty about the consequences of the litigation, vendors and donors may lose some degree of confidence in the organization, and cash flow may be impacted as legal fees mount. All of these consequences can be planned for by a nonprofit in order to ameliorate their most adverse effects.

This chapter gives nonprofit boards and executives a familiarity with the options available for resolving disputes — both to protect their nonprofit's assets and to assert their own claims against others where necessary.

CIVIL LITIGATION

Civil litigation, the most familiar type of dispute resolution, refers to a lawsuit or court proceeding and all of the events leading up to and following trial. It is well known that most lawsuits do not result in full trials on the merits, but are resolved at some earlier stage. What is less understood is that the time and effort leading up to trial is often as involved and important as the trial itself.

In addition to the simple model of civil plaintiff versus civil defendant, litigation may also include more complex multiparty cases, disputes with the government that go before administrative tribunals or boards of contract appeals, criminal matters, and other proceedings. Although this section discusses the more traditional plaintiff-versus-defendant model, the form and procedure is analogous in all such litigation.

In the United States, there are separate court systems in all 50 states. In addition, there is a separate system of federal courts. Each court system has its own rules and procedures. Although they are often very similar, there will be differences in limitations and deadlines, types of discovery, pleading rules, and other procedures. Experienced litigation counsel will be able to assist a nonprofit in navigating the rules and should be consulted as early in the process as possible.

COMMENCEMENT OF A LAWSUIT

The lawsuit formally begins with the filing of a complaint in a court of competent jurisdiction. The complaint must be "served" on the party being sued. For an organization, this usually means that the complaint and a summons are delivered directly to an officer of the organization, the organization's resident agent, or, in some circumstances, an agency of the state. Once the lawsuit is served, the sued party, called the defendant, has certain obligations, and the time for performing these duties begins to run with service.

Upon being served with the complaint and summons, the defendant should make a note of the date and time when the lawsuit was received in order to calculate the various deadlines that follow. Although the time for responding to a lawsuit varies from jurisdiction to jurisdiction, there will be some number of days in which the defendant must respond to the complaint. The consequence for failing to respond is possibly a default that may lead to a judgment being entered against the defendant.

The defendant must make certain important decisions upon receiving the lawsuit that will impact the course of the lawsuit from that point forward. Based on those decisions, the defendant will either file an answer, counterclaim or other claim, or a motion seeking immediate relief.

The options that must be evaluated upon receiving a complaint and summons include whether a preliminary motion should be filed to challenge the sufficiency of the complaint or the service of process, to dispute the jurisdiction of the court, or to raise other issues. The defendant should also evaluate whether it is entitled to and would benefit from removing or transferring the lawsuit to a different court or jurisdiction. A defendant may also have the right in a contract to compel the plaintiff to resolve the dispute through arbitration or other means. It is generally appropriate upon receiving the lawsuit to determine whether a demand should be made upon the defendant's insurance carrier for defense and indemnification. Additionally, in responding to or answering the complaint, many jurisdictions require that a jury demand be pled then, if at all, and any compulsory counterclaims be brought.

CHECKLIST FOR A NONPROFIT SERVED WITH LAWSUIT PAPERS

- ☐ Note the time, date, and means by which the lawsuit papers were "served" or delivered.

- ☐ Determine whether there is any insurance available or any third-party that may be ultimately responsible for the damages sought.

- ☐ Preserve any relevant documents or other evidence, such as the contracts in a business dispute.

- ☐ Contact counsel and/or the insurance company to advise on the timing and substance of the response to the complaint in order to avoid default.

Although many times one has little choice in the matter, it is generally preferable to be the plaintiff rather than the defendant, if for no other reason than to be able to decide whether and how to file the action in the first place. Perhaps the single most important question a potential plaintiff must ask is when the statute of limitations expires on its claim. Once limitations expire, the right to sue is forever lost. Limitations, particularly for certain statutory claims such as liens and government claims, may be measured only in days. Other limitations may be measured in years. Limitations usually begin to run when the events giving rise to the claim occur, and end on the day the lawsuit is filed. Limitations are extremely unforgiving, and should be evaluated early, even if the suit is never ultimately filed.

Other considerations for a potential plaintiff are the same as those of a defendant served with suit papers. The plaintiff must determine in which jurisdiction the suit may be brought, whether one forum is advantageous over another, whether to plead a jury trial, and precisely who should be sued. Prior to filing suit, the potential plaintiff should evaluate whether ADR is a condition precedent to filing suit or an option that may be employed.

DISCOVERY

After the complaint is filed and the defendant answers, a case moves into the discovery phase. Discovery refers to the exchange of documents and information between the parties in the lawsuit and with other people and organizations in order to develop the claims and defenses that are raised in the complaint, answer, and other related pleadings. Although it may seem counterintuitive to many first-time litigants, opposing parties are entitled to discover from each other all relevant documents (broadly defined) and information, not privileged, that is relevant to any claim or defense. The information sought to be discovered does not ultimately have to be admissible in a court, but is discoverable if it is reasonably likely to lead to the discovery of other admissible evidence. Certain privileges, most notably, the attorney-client privilege, may provide protection from discovery for some information, but generally, parties should anticipate a very broad obligation to provide information to the opposing party.

Depending on the local rules where the lawsuit is filed, discovery includes some variation of the following:

Initial Disclosures

In many federal and some state jurisdictions, parties will be required to provide initial disclosures. These often comprehensive disclosures must be made within a short time period after the initial pleadings are filed and do not require a request from the opposing party. In the federal courts, for example, initial disclosures include the names, addresses, and telephone numbers of all individuals likely to have discoverable information that a party may use to support its position, identification of all documents that a party may use to support its position, an estimate of each party's claimed damages, and copies of applicable insurance policies.

Interrogatories

Interrogatories are written questions served on the opposing party that must be answered in writing under oath. Courts usually limit the number of interrogatories that a party may propound to an opposing party. Answers must usually be made in 30 days and must be supplemented by the answering party if new or different information is obtained before trial. Although the answers will be signed by a single representative of an organization, they will usually contain information gathered from many people. Care must be exercised in responding to interrogatories because they are not only an exchange of potentially harmful information, but also may be used as evidence at trial or to contradict or impeach witnesses.

Requests for Production

Parties may also make requests for production of documents and things from the opposing party. The term "documents" is very broadly defined and includes such items as paper documents, audio and video tapes, and electronic files. Documents must usually be produced in the manner in which they are kept in the ordinary course of business or organized to correspond to the numbered requests from the requesting party. Depending on the type of dispute, the volume of documents exchanged could be a small stack of paper for a slip-and-fall lawsuit, or dozens of boxes of documents for a copyright infringement suit. The exchange of candid and voluminous e-mails has provided litigants with a treasure trove of useful information as well as a burden of information management.

Request for Admissions

Parties may also make requests for admissions to the opposing party. Those are numbered statements that the opposing party must affirm or deny, in writing, within a set period of time. The affirmation or denial has conclusive weight at trial. Failure to respond to a request for admissions is construed as an admission, and the knowing denial of a true statement may result in sanctions against the denying party.

Depositions

Perhaps the most effective discovery tool available to a litigant is the deposition. A deposition notice, accompanied by a subpoena, is essentially a court order that a person appear at a particular time and place to give testimony, produce documents, or both. Any person or organization with discoverable information may be deposed, unless the person is outside the subpoena power of the court or the party has already taken more than the number of depositions permitted by local court rules. A testimonial deposition is a verbal examination of a witness, usually in a lawyer's conference room, under oath. Depositions are transcribed, in real time, by a court reporter present at the deposition and are commonly videotaped for use at trial. The witness may appear with a lawyer, who may interpose objections to some questions, although the witness must answer all questions unless they amount to harassment or infringe on the attorney-client privilege.

Parties may also depose a nonprofit organization's representative, called the *corporate designee*, by serving with the deposition notice a list of topics that will be covered by the deposition. The corporate designee is a person or persons selected by the organization to speak on its behalf with respect to those topics identified. The testimony of the corporate designee does not have to be based on personal knowledge, but can be derived from an investigation by that designee into the matter. Corporate designee depositions have a legally binding effect on an organization concerning the matters set forth in the deposition notice. Often, a corporate designee deposition is taken of a nonparty solely for the purpose of obtaining documents. If a notice and subpoena for deposition solely for documents (known as a deposition *duces tecum*) is served, it is customary that the deponent need not appear if all of the documents are produced.

Organizations are often served with subpoenas in connection with lawsuits in which they are not a party. Nevertheless, they must comply with a properly issued and served subpoena. The subpoena will most likely demand that the organization produce documents or designate a representative to testify at deposition or at trial. Upon receiving a subpoena, the organization must quickly determine whether it intends to object to the subpoenas and, if not, what steps must be taken to comply, including preservation of any documents requested. Fortunately, courts provide certain protections for nonlitigants that are served with subpoenas. For instance, some jurisdictions provide that the party issuing the subpoena pay to the deponent travel or document production costs. Also, courts may protect parties from undue burden, such as excessive travel to testify. However, these objections must be raised in a timely manner or they may be waived.

TRIAL

The culmination of the litigation process is the court trial. Trials may be conducted with or without juries and can take anywhere from a few hours to several weeks. The time between filing a lawsuit and the commencement of trial varies widely from jurisdiction to jurisdiction and may also vary, depending upon the type of case within a particular jurisdiction. A lawsuit can come to trial in as little as a few months in certain "rocket docket" jurisdictions, or only after years have passed in other jurisdictions. Except in certain small-claims courts, organizations are prevented from entering an appearance or participating in a trial without legal representation.

Volumes have been written about how trials are conducted, but most trials consist of the following basic parts: opening statements by the lawyers, plaintiff's case (examining witnesses and introducing other evidence), the defendant(s)' case, any rebuttal case, and closing arguments by the lawyers. Peppered throughout these elements are various motions and other procedural happenings that may be unique to each case.

Trials may be decided by a jury or by the judge (a "bench trial"). Whether a trial is to be heard by a jury depends on two things. First, whether any party has a right to a jury trial. Second, whether a timely demand was made to exercise the right. Jury trials are usually longer and consume greater resources than bench trials. In addition to jury selection and disputes arising from jury instructions, the intensity of evidentiary disputes increases because of the importance of controlling what evidence the jury hears. Many believe that jury trials also result in more extreme and less predictable verdicts.

The primary purpose of a trial is to convince either the judge or the jury that one's cause is right and that one is entitled to the relief sought. Another significant purpose is to establish a record, through the admission of testimony and documentary evidence, upon which an appeals court may determine the correctness of the judge or the jury's decision. Even with the best and most prepared counsel, the outcome of a trial, especially with a jury, is never certain and appeals are always possible.

In most jurisdictions, a dissatisfied litigant has at least one appeal as of right available to it. Importantly, just because a litigant is dissatisfied does not necessarily mean that there are legitimate grounds for appeal. Typical trial court errors that are appealed include improper jury instructions, improper admission or nonadmission of evidence, and incorrect conclusions of law by the court.

ALTERNATIVE DISPUTE RESOLUTION (ADR)

Because of the expense, time, and complexity of the traditional court trial, many nonprofits are looking to ADR to resolve disagreements. There is no limit to the different types of ADR that may be employed, although they range along a spectrum between full adjudication of the dispute at one end and simple, nonbinding facilitation at the other. Disputes may be resolved through a binding decision by a third party or by the nonbinding assistance of a facilitator — or something in between. The most common forms of ADR are binding arbitration and nonbinding mediation, but other forms are available, such as minitrials, neutral fact-finding, and peer evaluation.

ARBITRATION

Arbitration is an out-of-court process in which the disputing parties, by agreement, submit their dispute to an arbitrator for decision. Although arbitrations generally include a hearing, they may also be decided on paper submissions.

Arbitration has advantages and disadvantages that distinguish it from court trials: Arbitrations are almost always privately conducted and result in decisions that are not necessarily made part of the public record. Because the arbitrator is selected by the parties, he or she will typically be an expert in the subject matter of the dispute (for example, health care, construction, employment law). As a result, the parties may often feel that a more just and reasonable result is achieved. Depending on the procedure selected, arbitrations may occur more quickly than a court trial and could be less expensive. (Some arbitrations may, in fact, be more expensive than a court trial if the parties agree to engage in the same level of discovery and preparation with an arbitrator; the arbitrator's fees and costs for hearing space must also be paid by the parties.) Finally, as discussed below, appeals from an arbitration decision are rare, making an arbitration award less subject to a costly appeal than a court judgment.

Arbitrations also differ from court trials in the extent of discovery. Arbitrations generally provide for much *less* discovery than a court trial. A typical arbitration proceeding may include a document exchange but no depositions or other discovery. Parties may agree to limit or expand discovery as they see fit, but there is no fundamental right to discovery under most arbitration law.

Arbitrations are necessarily conducted by agreement of the parties, either before or after the dispute has arisen. Often, parties to a contract will have included an arbitration clause in the agreement specifying that all disputes must be resolved by arbitration. Federal courts and the courts in most states will enforce an agreement to arbitrate and any resulting arbitration award. An arbitration contract clause may define the rules of the arbitration, the number or identity of arbitrators, and other considerations. There are also several well-regarded private organizations that will administer the arbitration for the parties for a fee.

Arbitration organizations offer standard contract language that specifies their organization as the agreed-upon administrator. One such clause provided by the American Arbitration Association (AAA) states:

> Any controversy or claim arising out of or relating to this contract, or the breach thereof, shall be settled by arbitration administered by the American Arbitration Association under its Commercial Arbitration Rules, and judgment on the award rendered by the arbitrator(s) may be entered into any court having jurisdiction thereof.

As is suggested by this model contract clause, the AAA has its own set of rules governing the conduct of the arbitration proceedings and it maintains a list of arbitrators.

Unlike the decision of a trial court, an arbitrator's decision is usually final. Any appeal of an arbitrator's award is in a state or federal court; however, the award will only be overturned, in most jurisdictions, under very narrow circumstances, such as fraud or corruption. Generally, an arbitrator's decision cannot be successfully appealed, even if the arbitrator has plainly made a mistake of fact or law.

MEDIATION

Mediation comes in a variety of forms, but is generally a voluntary, nonbinding dispute-resolution procedure. The parties appear before a mediator and the mediator assists the parties, through various means, in crafting a settlement. Given that mediation is nonbinding, there is no obligation for either party to reach a settlement and an unsuccessful mediation will often be followed by trial or arbitration.

Mediators may employ facilitative or evaluative methods, or something in between. Mediators who focus on facilitation generally avoid offering a decision or conclusion as to how the matter ought to be resolved, but they skillfully insert themselves in the dialogue between the parties to assist them in crafting their own solution. Mediators who are more evaluative tend to act more as arbitrators in that they hear each party's case and reach a decision. However, that conclusion is a nonbinding, though often persuasive, evaluation.

Parties may arrive at mediation by consensus, court order, or other means. Even court-ordered mediations are often successful despite their nonbinding character. Successful mediation participants approach the mediation with greater flexibility than they do the litigation that may follow. Among other things, the mediation participants should focus their energy on communicating directly with the opposing party, not simply attempting to convince the mediator of its position. The mediation time should be taken advantage of because often once a lawsuit is filed, meaningful communication between parties slows down considerably.

Although there is no set procedure for mediation, mediations in the United States commonly follow a generally accepted format. Usually, each party takes a turn briefly presenting its side of the case. The presentations are generally offered without interruption by the opposing side, depending on the agreement of the parties and the discretion of the mediator. The mediator may ask questions during the initial presentation or may moderate the presentations as necessary. Following the presentations, and depending on the mediator's view of the parties' ability to communicate with each other, there may be an open negotiation session moderated by the mediator. In other cases, the mediator may choose to remove the parties to separate rooms and engage in "shuttle diplomacy." The mediator then moves back and forth between rooms in an attempt to achieve consensus on all or parts of the dispute. It is not uncommon for mediators using shuttle diplomacy to bring the lawyers, the principals, or other consultants together to discuss particular issues or to clarify certain facts.

The mediator may stay involved in the settlement process even after the formal mediation is complete. During the process, the mediator will emphasize the benefits of settlement including avoiding a public result, eliminating risks of outcome, removing uncertainty in collecting an award, and allowing the parties to focus on their core business rather than litigating past events. It has often been stated that a successful settlement is one where all parties leave a little unhappy. That is not necessarily the case, but the settlement does eliminate the risk of *great* unhappiness for either party in the result.

The criteria for selecting a mediator are very different from those for selecting an arbitrator. Because an arbitrator is engaged to render a binding decision, an arbitrator should be chosen primarily based on his or her expertise and experience, as well as impartiality. A mediator is not expected to reach a binding decision, so the most important characteristic of a mediator is his or her style and ability to mediate, conciliate, and communicate. Depending on the nature of the dispute, a mediator with a strong ability to facilitate communication between the parties may be preferable. In other circumstances, one with good "arm twisting" abilities may be better. Although there are differing views on the matter, it may also be preferable to have a mediator well versed in the subject matter of the dispute.

Mediations, because they are voluntary, are generally final. Successful mediations will result in a written settlement agreement outlining the terms, including any money to be paid or received, the dismissal of lawsuits, the extent of confidentiality, and any other considerations on which there is agreement.

MEDIATION VS. ARBITRATION

The question of whether to use mediation or arbitration is often determined by the nature of the dispute. If the case involves a contract, there will frequently be a provision in the agreement specifying that dispute resolution is to take place by arbitration, in which case it is required. In those cases where the method of dispute resolution has not been mandated, the parties can choose the approach they feel is most likely to be successful. Mediation may be more attractive where the parties have been unable to resolve matters themselves, but could reasonably be expected to achieve success with the help and intervention of an unbiased and knowledgeable mediator. Where emotion, stubbornness, or other strong emotions are in play among the parties, arbitration may be the best alternative to litigation.

OTHER TYPES OF ADR

Although mediation and arbitration are the most common forms of alternative dispute resolution, they are by no means the only ones. Methods of resolving disputes are limited only by the creativity of the parties. Some other common alternative ADR methods include neutral fact-finding, peer evaluation, and mini-trials. Wherever possible, organizations entering into contracts should include provisions in the contract for their preferred dispute resolution method. The type of dispute resolution should be tailored to the needs of the parties and the types of anticipated disputes. Parties may even agree to establish a private dispute resolution board (DRB) for ongoing projects. The DRB can, in addition to resolving disputes, assist in fostering a sense of partnering between joint venturers having an ongoing relationship.

Chapter Q&As

Q: What can a nonprofit organization do to keep from being sued?

A: The American jurisprudence system provides liberal opportunities for aggrieved parties to bring a lawsuit to pursue remedies for their claims. As a result, if a party is determined to file a lawsuit against a nonprofit organization, there is little the organization can do to stop this. It must rely, instead, on an adequate defense to the suit. There are, however, certain risk management strategies available to a nonprofit organization to minimize its risk of being sued. These include such things as consistent treatment of slip-and-fall accidents, the use of clear written agreements with others for their services to the organization, early communication with parties who have raised potential claims, consistent application of fair personnel policies, and careful monitoring of regulatory compliance.

Q: What is the difference between arbitration and mediation?

A: Arbitration and mediation, also known as alternative dispute resolution, are mechanisms for parties to resolve their differences short of full-blown litigation. Arbitration is an out-of-court process in which the disputing parties, by agreement, submit the dispute to an arbitrator for decision. Although arbitrations generally include a hearing, they may also be decided on paper submissions. Arbitrations are necessarily conducted by agreement of the parties, either before or after the dispute has arisen. Mediation comes in a variety of forms, but it is generally a voluntary, nonbinding dispute-resolution procedure. The parties appear before a mediator and the mediator assists the parties, through various means, in crafting a settlement. Since the mediation is nonbinding, there is no obligation for either party to reach a settlement and an unsuccessful mediation will often be followed by a trial or arbitration.

It is not news that we live in a litigious society. There was a time when nonprofit organizations received the benefit of charitable immunity and were seldom the target of litigation. That time has passed. Nonprofits are now frequently the subject of lawsuits and boards of directors must be prepared to aggressively defend the organization against such suits. Likewise, boards must be prepared to institute litigation to protect their nonprofit's assets, to seek redress for damages suffered by the constituencies they serve, and to pursue advocacy objectives. At the same time, the chief executive should maintain an effective risk management program that can help to minimize the organization's exposure to lawsuits. When a dispute is inevitable, the organization should consider the option of alternative dispute resolution mechanisms such as arbitration and mediation, which are generally more efficient and less costly, before proceeding to litigation in court.

Questions the Board Should Ask

- Does our organization have an effective risk-management program?

- Do our major contracts contain alternative dispute resolution clauses as an option to or instead of litigation?

- Is the board regularly apprised by management or counsel of litigation against the organization?

- Are there any litigation trends in our field that we should be aware of?

Appendix I: The Federal Form 990*

A TOUR OF THE FORM 990

This section takes readers through the essentials of the IRS Form 990. It breaks down each part of the form and highlights the information required, the potential problems in completing each section, and the potential opportunities to educate the public. Readers should note that the provisions described below are revised periodically by the IRS. For a complete set of instructions and the current year's forms, visit the IRS Web site at www.irs.gov/eo.

MISCELLANEOUS INFORMATION

Information Required: Basic information such as name, address, federal identification number, type of exemption, and accounting method are included here.

Potential Problems: If the organization has moved, be sure to correct the address or check the change of address box. Also, make sure you fill out the organization's federal identification number correctly. If it is incorrect, the IRS will not know that the organization has filed and may send penalty notices. Double check that the code section for exemption is correct [e.g., 501(c)(4) instead of 501(c)(3)].

Potential Opportunities To Educate: None in this section.

PART I: REVENUE, EXPENSES, AND CHANGES IN NET ASSETS OR FUND BALANCES

Information Required: Most of this portion is a summary of detailed information presented in Parts II, IV, and VII with references to particular lines. Items not appearing elsewhere are contributions or grants (general, indirect, and government) broken down into cash and noncash amounts. Also included are summaries of rental income/expense, security/asset sales, special events revenue/expense, and income from inventory sales. A schedule of contributors of $5,000 or more (of "money, securities, or other property") must be attached on all copies except the public inspection copies. For tax years beginning after 1999, the list of contributors is included on Schedule B, which attaches to the 990. Detailed schedules are also required for rental income, sale of assets, special events, and inventory sales. At the end of this section is a summary of changes in net assets (previously called "fund balance") showing net income, beginning net assets, other changes in net assets, and ending net assets. Other changes in net assets require a statement to be attached. Since unrealized gains (or losses) on securities are not reported as income on the 990, most organizations with investments in securities will have some amount on this line with that explanation.

Potential Problems: Potential problems for this section include issues such as not attaching all required schedules and statements; leaving the schedule of contributors (or Schedule B) attached to the public inspection copy or copy posted to the

---

*Reprinted from *The IRS Form 990: A Window into Nonprofits*, by Andrew S. Lang and Michael Sorrells. Washington, DC: BoardSource, 2001.

Internet; and not including full names, addresses, and amounts on the schedule of contributors or Schedule B (government grants do not have to be included on the attached schedule). Another potential problem is when amounts on referenced lines do not agree with the line on another part of the 990 that is referenced (this normally will not occur on forms prepared with professional tax software, but is seen frequently on forms prepared by hand).

Potential Opportunities To Educate: Most of this section is straightforward, with accuracy and completeness being the goal. However, if there are other changes in net assets (line 20) other than unrealized gains or losses, it is possible to put them in a better light with a meaningful explanation. Instead of "prior period adjustment"— an explanation that could be a cover-up for a major mistake — it would sound much better to tell the reader why there was an adjustment (e.g., adjustment to beginning liabilities).

PART II: STATEMENT OF FUNCTIONAL EXPENSES

Information Required: Part II is a breakdown of the organization's expenses by "natural" category. By natural, we mean expense lines such as payroll, travel expenses, printing, etc., and not simply a breakdown of expenses by program (as most audited exempt organization financial statements provide). There are four columns for most of the expenses listed: total, program services, management and general, and fundraising. Thus, a particular expense might be broken down into as many as three different components. Only 501(c)(3) charitable organizations and (c)(4) social welfare organizations are required to fill out all four columns. Other organizations such as 501(c)(6) trade and professional associations are required to fill in only the total column — the other three columns are optional for them. There are 21 lines for standard categories of expenses in Part II and an additional line for other expenses that are required to be itemized. Detailed schedules are required for grants and allocations and assistance provided to individuals as well as for depreciation expense.

Potential Problems: For a 501(c)(3) or (c)(4) organization, the reader can easily tell how much of the total expenditures goes toward programs and how much is spent on fundraising and administrative expenses. If an organization's 990 reports a low amount of spending on programs, a prospective donor might be persuaded to give money to an organization reporting higher program expenses even though the organization might have a valid reason for the high fundraising or administrative expenditures. In addition, watchdog organizations use this part of the 990 for a large part of their ratings calculations, which they publish and upon which they base their recommendations. Finally, extremely low program expenditure levels over a period of years could cause concern on the part of the IRS as to whether the organization should maintain its exempt status. Board members should pay close attention and ask questions when the levels of expenditures appear to be askew.

Potential Opportunities To Educate: If the management and general expenditures appear too high, it may be simply a case of the organization not allocating as much as is permitted of these expenditures as overhead to its programs. The organization may wish to consult with an outside accountant experienced with nonprofits in order to determine that it is maximizing its allocation of overhead.

We mentioned above that it is optional for 501(c)(6) trade associations to fill in any columns other than the "total" column. For the well-run organization with low overhead and significant program services, it may be a good option to take. Disclosing such favorable information could help with membership and would certainly be a plus when under any public scrutiny.

PART III: STATEMENT OF PROGRAM SERVICE ACCOMPLISHMENTS

Information Required: Part III is closely related to Part II, but most of the information is in narrative form. The first line in this part asks for the organization's primary exempt purpose. Next, the organization must describe its four largest exempt program achievements and then list any other programs. There is no requirement that the information fit on the few lines the form allows for the descriptions — many organizations put the majority of the information on attached schedules and reference them on Part III. Additionally, 501(c)(3) and (c)(4) organizations are required to disclose the amounts they spend on each program listed. Total program expenditures disclosed should agree with the totals from Part II. Just as in Part II, organizations other than 501(c)(3) or (c)(4) organizations have the option of disclosing these program expenses.

Potential Problems: The biggest risk in this part is that of providing a program description, or overall exempt purpose description, that is not in keeping with the exempt purpose for which the organization was granted its tax exemption in the first place. For example, a 501(c)(3) organization whose program description only indicates benefits for members sounds more like a trade association exempt under 501(c)(6) than a legitimate 501(c)(3) charity. If the IRS were to discover this, either through examining the return or because of a third-party complaint, it could revoke the organization's 501(c)(3) charitable status.

Potential Opportunities To Educate: This is probably the best part of the Form 990 for actually telling the reader what your organization is all about. Most organizations miss the opportunity and just describe their exempt purpose and major programs in one or two terse, fairly general lines. While this may satisfy the IRS, it doesn't really give the reader any idea of the breadth and scope of the valuable work in which the organization is engaged. The proactive organization will carefully craft comprehensive statements about its programs including (in addition to complete descriptions) measurable accomplishments such as number of clients served, circulation of publications, number of members, etc. Nonmeasurable accomplishments also should be fully described. This could include milestones attained and completion of phases. The future goals of a program also could be touched upon (this would be especially important for a program that is in its infancy). One caveat: Be sure that the statements do not embellish the truth — that could create problems way out of proportion with any goodwill attained.

As mentioned above, the 501(c)(6) or trade association has the option in this part to disclose how much it spends on particular programs. It is easy to see that such disclosure might be advantageous to the organization that is proud of what it expends on its more significant programs and wants to tout its spending priorities.

The nonprofit that spends time carefully considering and developing what it reports in Part III will be clearly presenting useful and, hopefully, positive information to the reader.

Part IV: Balance Sheets

Information Required: This part is a reiteration of the balance sheet information from the organization's financial statements for the current and prior years, presented in a slightly different format with certain items broken down in different detail than on the financials. Many of the lines require attachments that provide detail for the totals on the line. Of particular note are lines requiring details of loans both to and from officers, directors, and key employees of the organization. The attachments should disclose the individual's name, relationship to the organization, and the loan terms.

Potential Problems: First and foremost, these balance sheets should agree with the published financial statements. If they do not, the organization is not filing a complete and accurate return and could be subject to penalties. The easy way to check for agreement is to simply compare the total assets and liabilities for agreement with the financial statement totals instead of trying to check each line. (One possible reason why the totals might not agree would be if the financial statements are consolidated with those of affiliates. The Form 990 is not usually consolidated.) Second, any line requiring further detail should have an attached schedule. Lack of a required schedule is an incomplete filing.

The aforementioned officer/director loan schedules have the potential to highlight serious problems. Below-market loans made to an officer, or above-market loans made from an officer to the organization, can open the organization to private inurement issues, which will endanger the tax-exempt status. With 501(c)(3) or (c)(4) organizations, such loan terms can be considered a "private benefit transaction" that can cause heavy excise taxes to be levied against both the board member and the organization's managers (including, in some cases, board members) who approved the transaction. While there may be legitimate reasons for loans to and from board members, they must be conducted at arm's length.

Potential Opportunities To Educate: There are no significant opportunities to include additional information on the balance sheet. The organization's relative financial health (or lack thereof) as shown on the balance sheet will be apparent to the savvy reader.

Parts IV-A and IV-B: Reconciliation of Revenue Expenses

Information Required: This section should be completed if the organization has audited financial statements — otherwise it is left blank. Its purpose is to show the reader the differences between the total revenue and expenses on the audited financial statement and the totals as reported on the Form 990. Some of these differences are simply due to certain items of income and expenses not being reported on the 990 that are reported on the financials (and vice versa). For example, unrealized gains and donated services are usually reported on audited financial statements but never on the 990. Other differences are simply due to certain items being netted differently on each of the forms (in these cases, the same item will be an adjustment to both income and expense).

Potential Problems: This is another test for completeness. If the beginning lines do not agree with revenue and expenses on the audited financial statement, then the return may be incomplete. Second (assuming the first line is correct), if the last line on each of the schedules does not agree with the total revenue and expenses as reported on page 1 of the Form 990, then the reconciling items are misstated or the entries on the return are incorrect. This would indicate a sloppy job in preparation. This kind of imbalance is much more likely to occur on a handwritten or typed return than one prepared with professional software.

Potential Opportunities To Educate: None in this section.

PART V: LIST OF OFFICERS, DIRECTORS, TRUSTEES, AND KEY EMPLOYEES

Information Required: This list must include all of the above individuals with their compensation for the year, the organization's contributions to their benefit plans and deferred compensation, and expense allowances paid. Noncompensated board members also must be listed and shown with zero compensation (it is common for the compensated personnel to be listed in Part V with an attachment referenced for the noncompensated board members who are then listed on a separate schedule). "Key" employees for the purposes of this part are employees with significant responsibility and authority within the organization. Typically, chief executives, chief operating officers, and chief financial officers fall into this category; personnel responsible for a segment of the organization, such as program managers, usually are not considered key employees for this part of the 990.

A question at the end of Part V requires the organization to disclose anyone on the above list who is paid a total of more than $100,000 by the organization and/or any related organization(s). This typically covers the situation where the chief executive of a foundation is paid by a separate parent organization. The IRS evidently wants the reader to know the total compensation that the chief executive is receiving, or alternatively, that he or she is not really serving as a volunteer. If the chief executive is paid by a management company, that too has to be reported.

Potential Problems: The first problem here is the organization's (and management's) natural reluctance to publicize the salaries of its executives. Chief executives and board members coming from private industry especially have a hard time understanding that this disclosure is part of the price of having tax-exempt status. It is not sufficient to print a statement saying that "salary information is available upon request," and the organization cannot omit the salary information from the public disclosure copies it disseminates or publishes on the Internet. Thus, as tough as it may seem, the organization must fully disclose complete salary and benefit information. While the list asks for addresses of the officers, it is not necessary — or recommended — to list home addresses on this form. The organization's address or the individual's business address is sufficient.

Deferred compensation, such as 401(k) or 403(b) savings plans, must be included in the benefits total when it is accrued, even though it may not go on the individual's W-2 until it is paid. Since many chief executives receive substantial deferred compensation each year, if the total compensation on Part V is not reported, it will be greatly understated. For example, an executive director whose contract calls for a salary of $50,000 and contributions to a deferred savings plan of an additional $25,000 per year has really received $75,000 of compensation, not just the $50,000 actually paid that year.

501(c)(3) or (c)(4) organizations that pay a substantial total compensation package to its executives (salary plus benefits) can face additional exposure. If the IRS determines that compensation is "excessive," it can assess stiff excise taxes on the compensated individual and on the organization's managers (including board members) who approved the arrangement. In making the determination of whether there is excessive compensation, the IRS looks at the facts and circumstances. There are a number of circumstances that can justify a salary that, on the surface, appears excessive. For example, perhaps the organization is considerably more complex to run than most other organizations of its size; or maybe the executive is required to have specific advanced technical knowledge, such as of some medical or scientific discipline. If executive salaries appear to be high, the board may want to consult with outside advisers on procedures for establishing salary guidelines and ensuring a "presumption of reasonableness."

Potential Opportunities To Educate: Some organizations choose to attach a statement explaining how its chief executive's salary was established. Such statements may discuss the extensive job search undertaken to find this person, how the salary was negotiated, or that the salary is comparable to those of executives in similar-sized nonprofits or at the organization from which the executive was recruited. Such a statement may calm down a reader whose first reaction is righteous indignation to a salary that might be higher than that of the U.S. president. The IRS encourages organizations to attach explanations when an officer receives an unusual payment (e.g., a large severance payment) that would otherwise raise eyebrows. Since Part V is a major focus for the news media and the public, anything explaining what appears to be excessive should be considered for inclusion in the return.

PART VI: OTHER INFORMATION

Information Required: Part VI is mostly a series of yes or no questions that run a wide gamut. Some of them have the potential to cause problems if they are not answered correctly. All of them must be answered — yes, no, or not applicable.

Potential Problems: Question 77 asks if there were changes to the organizing or governing documents during the year. If the answer is yes, be sure that a copy of the new document is attached along with a signed statement certifying it. If there was a dissolution or liquidation (often the case when there is a merger), answer yes to question 79 and attach a statement explaining the situation and copies of the legal documentation.

If any amount is entered on line 81(a), concerning political activity, by a 501(c)(3), it would indicate that the organization's exemption is in jeopardy. A yes answer by most other types of organizations would indicate the organization might have to file a Form 1120-POL and perhaps pay tax on the political expenditures. Question 85 should be filled in by 501(c)(4), (c)(5), and (c)(6) organizations that engage in lobbying activities. Not filling this in properly could cause such organizations to be subject to a 35 percent proxy tax on lobbying expenditures. Keep in mind that there is a difference between political activity and lobbying. Nonprofits are allowed to lobby to a certain extent. They are not, however, allowed any political activity, such as contributing to campaigns.

Question 89 is a series of questions for 501(c)(3) or (c)(4) organizations concerning excess benefit transactions — transactions in which an improper financial benefit is received by someone who is an "insider" to the organization such as a chief executive or board member — and any penalty taxes that may have been paid because of them during the year. If any dollar amounts are filled in, or 89b is answered yes, the board ought to know exactly what happened and how it is being handled.

Potential Opportunities To Educate: No obvious opportunities in this section.

PART VII: ANALYSIS OF INCOME-PRODUCING ACTIVITIES

Information Required: In this section, all income except contributions and grants (see Part I) is reported and categorized. At the top of the page, the organization lists the revenue streams from various programs (e.g., publications, conferences, services to members) and categorizes them into three columns: unrelated taxable income (income from business activities that are not related to the organization's exempt purpose), unrelated income that is excluded from tax by law, and income that is related to the organization's exempt purpose. Going down the form there are lines for specific income streams including membership dues and investment income. Each item of unrelated taxable income should have a business code preceding it; similarly, excluded income should be preceded by an exclusion code. Exclusion codes may be found in the full instructions to the Form 990, available at www.irs.gov.

Potential Problems: The total of Part VII when added to total contributions and grants should agree with line 12 (total revenue) on Part I. If it does not, incomplete or incorrect information is being furnished. This kind of imbalance is again more likely to be seen on a handwritten or typed return than on one prepared with professional software. All lines requiring a code should have one. Large dollar amounts labeled as "miscellaneous" or "other" raise questions as to what might be hidden. The information needed to prepare this section should be available from the organization's normal accounting records.

Potential Opportunities To Educate: The best tactic here is to break down the revenue streams instead of lumping programs together. This way, in Part VIII (below), more descriptions can be provided.

PART VIII: RELATIONSHIP OF ACTIVITIES TO THE ACCOMPLISHMENT OF EXEMPT PURPOSES

Information Required: In this section, an explanation must be supplied for each amount reported in Part VII, Column E, "Related or Exempt Function Income." This narrative should describe how each activity contributed to the accomplishment of exempt purposes. Every line with an amount reported as "related" in Part VII, Column E, must have its own explanation. For example, if seminar registration fees are one of the amounts reported in Part VII, Column E, then the obvious explanation would be something like "Seminars provide members and the general public with important learning opportunities on the subject of XYZ. The latest developments are discussed, and innovative solutions to current problems are brought to these forums."

Potential Problems: A common mistake made by many organizations is to simply state in this part how the funds were used. That monies are used for an exempt purpose does not, in and of itself, turn an unrelated activity into a related one. For example, a fundraising gala to raise money for a charity's programs is not usually a related activity even though its cause may be noble. Such a gala is really an unrelated activity (but will usually avoid being taxed because it fits one of the exclusions that we talked about in the Part VII discussion). Thus, incorrect explanations in this part could lead the reader (and the IRS) to conclude that some of the related income reported might actually be unrelated and thus potentially taxable.

Potential Opportunities To Educate: As with Part III, this is an ideal section to let the organization shine. Each stream of revenue (again, be sure that they are not lumped together in Part VII) can be described on attached statements with sufficient detail to show the magnitude, scope, and purpose. For example, the statement about the organization's seminars could be expanded to read something like "Regional seminars were conducted in 14 cities throughout the United States. Instructors were faculty members from major universities. The 2,850 participants had the opportunity to expand their knowledge by learning about the history and economics of XYZ. Additionally, such programs provide a forum for discussion of potential issues facing XYZ in the decades to come." Several statements such as this would really allow the organization to put its best foot forward and fully inform the reader about exactly what the organization does.

PART IX: INFORMATION REGARDING TAXABLE SUBSIDIARIES AND DISREGARDED ENTITIES

Information Required: Some nonprofit organizations own for-profit subsidiaries. These might be organizations whose stock was once received as a gift and is being kept as an investment, or for-profit subsidiaries created by the nonprofit to conduct business to raise funds for the organization. This straightforward section asks for a minimal amount of information concerning income, activities, and ending assets as well as the name of the subsidiary and its federal ID number.

Potential Problems: One of the questions on Part VI asks if the organization owns a taxable subsidiary. If that question is answered yes, then Part IX must be completed. The IRS wants information about subsidiaries because there are special rules concerning possible unrelated business income from such relationships; it also is concerned that relations between the two are at arm's length to avoid private inurement that could jeopardize the nonprofit organization's tax exemption. If there are taxable subsidiaries, it is good to be familiar with these rules.

Potential Opportunities To Educate: None in this section.

PART X: INFORMATION REGARDING TRANSFERS ASSOCIATED WITH PERSONAL BENEFIT CONTRACTS

Information Required: This section of the 990 was added for taxable years beginning after 1999. In the late 1990s, several variations of split-dollar life insurance contribution schemes began being marketed to donors as a way to make a charitable contribution without really giving much to the organization. In response, Congress added new code section 170(f)(10). This section not only prohibits the charitable deduction for transfers associated with split-dollar arrangements (arrangements where both the charity and the donor stand to benefit from the arrangement — usually in the form of a life insurance policy), but also charges an excise tax to organizations paying premiums on such contracts. The new Part X of Form 990 identifies those organizations that have engaged in such activities and that should file excise tax returns.

Potential Problems: First of all, if this section is filled in, one may question the knowledge and/or prudence of management of the organization simply due to the fact that it allowed the organization to get involved in personal benefit contracts. Second, if Part X is filled in, board members must ensure that the excise tax returns and other reports are prepared properly. Finally, a board member who knows of split-dollar arrangements should step up if the organization has not reported it on the 990; to do otherwise is to condone fraudulent filing.

Potential Opportunities To Educate: None in this section.

A Tour of Schedule A

This brief tour guides readers through Schedule A, the mandatory attachment to the Form 990 for all 501(c)(3) organizations. Schedule A is a six-page attachment required to be completed by all 501(c)(3) charitable organizations. It is part of the Form 990 and, as such, is subject to public inspection. Since donations to these organizations qualify as a charitable tax deduction, the IRS wants some additional information to be sure they are continuing to qualify for this level of public trust. While many of the items in Schedule A will not be applicable to a particular organization, it is important to respond to all of the questions and to mark such questions as "n/a." There are no opportunities to educate the public on Schedule A information, so this section will focus on the more sensitive areas on this schedule and try to show what can help and hurt the charitable organization.

Parts I and II: Compensation of the Five Highest Paid Employees and Independent Contractors

The five highest compensated employees not included on the 990 Part V list of officers, directors, and key employees must be listed in this section with compensation and benefits information just as in Part V. Employees with salaries of less than $50,000 are not required to be listed. Again, the IRS and interested readers could make inferences as to excessive compensation from what is disclosed in this section. Additionally, the organization must list the five highest paid independent contractors ($50,000 or more) that it paid for professional services. This may include printers, accountants, or consultants. This provides the IRS with information as to whom the organization is paying significant sums. Large payments to contractors known to be professional fundraisers may be compared to fundraising expenses reported on the Form 990 to see if the amount of fundraising expenses reported is adequate.

Part III: Statements about Activities

Part III presents a set of questions about lobbying activities, various financial transactions with related individuals (such as board members), and grant activities. All of these questions must be answered yes or no. A yes to the lobbying question (line 1) means that Part VI of Schedule A must be completed.

Yes to most of the other questions requires explanations to be attached. Pay particular attention to descriptions and terms of loans and asset sales to and from related individuals. Remember that an arm's-length standard must be applied to such transactions: anything else has at least the appearance of a private inurement or a private benefit transaction that can spell exemption problems for the organization or excise taxes for the individuals involved.

If the organization discloses here that it gives grants, etc., to individuals or organizations, it must disclose a statement as to how it determines who receives the awards. Many organizations attach fairly detailed information (often gleaned from their own literature announcing their awards) that clearly illustrates that awards are given on merit and not on any kind of favoritism.

Part IV: Reason for Nonprivate Foundation Status

A box must be checked in this section. Most 501(c)(3) associations will be checking box 11a, 12, or 13 out of the several choices available. Which box is checked determines the support test (if any) that the organization must meet to retain its status as a public charity rather than a private foundation — a classification that subjects the organization to more restrictions on its activities than if it could qualify as a public charity. Usually, the determination letter that the organization received when it was granted its 501(c)(3) status will govern the box that is checked. A support organization (box 13) must provide information about the organization (or organizations) it supports.

Part IV-A: Support Schedule

The Support Schedule is the most complicated part of the form. Board members should be careful in reviewing this section, as it is quite technical. For complete instructions on this section, visit the IRS Web site at www.irs.gov. This part is required for organizations that checked box 10, 11, or 12 in Part IV (above). Other organizations do not fill in this schedule of support for the past four years. Organizations that checked box 10 or 11 must pass a support test, which is calculated on line 26, while box 12 organizations use the test calculated on line 27.

The box 10 or 11 organization's public support percentage on line 26f should be higher than 33⅓ percent. A schedule of excess contributors (if any) must be attached — this attachment is not open to public inspection since it lists contributors. Excess contributions are defined as contributions or grants from one source that are greater than 2 percent of the total contributions received by the organization for the four-year test period.

Organizations that fall under box 12 must have both a public support percentage greater than 33⅓ percent and an investment income percentage less than 33⅓ percent on lines 27e and 27h, respectively. These percentages are calculated after eliminating certain income items from "disqualified persons" and from persons who gave the organization more than 1 percent of its total support. Again, a schedule of any such persons must be attached to the return.

There is an exception for certain "unusual" grants received by any of the organizations required to complete the support schedule. An unusual grant is generally a large, one-time grant that the organization did not expect to receive (a typical example would be a large bequest from an estate). Unusual grants may be excluded from both the numerator and denominator of the support fraction, thus allowing the organization to receive such windfalls without injury to its support status.

If these public support percentages are not met, the organization's status as a public charity may be in jeopardy. Management should consult with its outside advisers in this situation for remediation.

PARTS VI-A AND VI-B: LOBBYING EXPENDITURES

Any 501(c)(3) organization that has engaged in any amount of lobbying has to fill out Part VI-A or VI-B. Organizations that have elected for "safe harbor" lobbying status (see definition below) fill out Part A, and those that haven't fill out Part B. The tax code says that charities cannot engage in "substantial" lobbying but then fails to define substantial. Charities that engage in substantial lobbying may lose their tax-exempt status.

Congress created the safe harbor election [501(h)] so that charities could expend certain amounts (based upon their total expenditures) on lobbying without being considered as doing substantial lobbying. Nonelecting organizations that participate in lobbying activities hold the burden of proof with the IRS in showing that its lobbying is not substantial. Thus, if Part VI-B is filled in, board members should ask management why it is risking its exempt status by not making this election. There are few cases where it would make sense not to do so.

PART VII: INFORMATION REGARDING TRANSACTIONS AND RELATIONSHIPS WITH NONCHARITABLE EXEMPT ORGANIZATIONS

This part asks for specifics about any financial dealings between 501(c)(3) organizations and other tax-exempt organizations. Transactions to be disclosed include cash/asset transfers, loans, reimbursement arrangements, purchase of assets, and performance of services. These kinds of arrangements are typical in the situation where a 501(c)(6) trade association has an affiliated 501(c)(3) foundation.

Because the charitable organization has a legal obligation to use its funds for only charitable purposes, the IRS is concerned that transactions between tax-exempt affiliated charitable and noncharitable organizations not give any kind of favor to the noncharitable organization. This part of the Schedule A should explain these transactions and may give the IRS some hints as to what it might want to look at. For example, a grant from a 501(c)(3) to (c)(6) has to be done within strict parameters or it will endanger the exempt status of the charity. In another common situation, the charity may pay the related parent organization a management fee for its administrative services. This would raise questions about whether the charity was paying fair market value for these services and could also cause unrelated business income concerns for the parent organization.

Appendix II: Glossary of Terms

401(k) Plan — salary-reduction agreement to provide tax-deferred income to participating employee

403(b) Plan — tax-sheltered annuity retirement plan for employees of 501(c)(3) organizations, usually with contributions made by the employee and employer

457 Deferred Compensation Plan — benefit plan specifically designed for executives and key employees

501(c)(3) — tax-exempt status defining public charities and private foundations

501(c)(4) — tax-exempt status defining social welfare organizations

501(c)(6) — tax-exempt status defining mainly trade and professional associations

501(h) election — option for public charities (except churches) to measure their permissible lobbying activity using an expenditure test

Advocacy — active positioning on a point of view or a plan for action

Age Discrimination in Employment Act (ADEA) — federal regulation prohibiting employment-related discrimination against employees over the age of 40

Alternative Dispute Resolution (ADR) — method by which legal conflicts and disputes are resolved privately outside of litigation in the public courts

Americans with Disabilities Act (ADA) — federal regulation prohibiting employment-related discrimination against a "qualified individual" with a disability when the discrimination is based on this disability

Antitrust laws — federal and state laws advancing and protecting competition in the marketplace

Arbitration — process where disputes are settled by an impartial third party (arbitrator) chosen by the disputing parties who agree in advance to abide by the final decision

Arm's-length transaction — a transaction negotiated by unrelated parties acting in their own self-interest

Articles of incorporation — document filed with a state agency to establish a corporation

Attorney General — chief legal officer of federal or state government

Audit — review of the books, records, and operations of the organization by independent accounting professionals

Board of directors — the governing body of an organization

Bylaws — legal document outlining the guidelines for governing the nonprofit organization

Charitable contribution — monetary or in-kind gift to a tax-exempt organization that is able to accept tax-deductible contributions

Charitable organization — a 501(c)(3) tax-exempt organization whose mission focuses on relief of poverty and suffering, education, advancement of religion, promotion of health, or other activities that benefit the general public and lessen the burden of the government

Charter — see articles of incorporation

Civil litigation — lawsuit that can be undertaken by individuals or organizations, seeking to reclaim what is owed to them

Civil Rights Act of 1964 — protection for employees from illegal employment decisions based on race, color, sex, religion, and ethnic background

Civil Rights Act of 1991 — amendment to the Civil Rights Act of 1964, including provision for damages in cases of intentional employment discrimination

Clayton Act — law prohibiting actions not addressed in the Sherman Act that try to curb competition or create a monopoly, specifically addressing mergers and acquisitions

Conflict of interest — situation where a person is on both sides of a financial transaction or decision making, providing and receiving benefits at the same time

Cooperative — organization for the benefit of members, where members make decisions, share labor, and profit from the actions

Copyright — legal protection for the authors and owners of "original works of authorship"

Corporate sponsorship — financial support provided by a for-profit corporation for specified activities of a nonprofit

Corporation — legal entity governed by state law and protecting affiliated investors from personal liability

Cy pres — doctrine permitting courts to interpret documents as closely as possible to their original intent

D&O (directors' and officers') insurance — liability insurance providing coverage for board members against various civil law violations

Deferred compensation — compensation not available until a later date

Defined benefit pension plan — benefit plan based on an employee's compensation and years of service

Defined contribution pension plan — benefit plan based on a fixed contribution formula

Deposition — a litigation device where one party asks questions of the other party or of a witness under oath

Determination letter — document provided by the IRS to recognize the tax-exempt status of a nonprofit organization

Disqualified person — IRS definition of a person with the ability to substantially influence or control the organization and who generally has a personal interest in the outcome of a decision

Duty of care — expectation for a board member to perform his or her duties in good faith and with the care that an ordinary prudent person in a like position would use under similar circumstances

Duty of loyalty — expectation for a board member to act in a manner he or she believes to be in the best interest of the organization

Duty of obedience — expectation for the board to keep the organization faithful to its mission

Electioneering — opposition, endorsement, working for or against, directly or indirectly, a candidate in a political campaign for public office

Electronic Communications Privacy Act (ECPA) — provisions for access, use, disclosure, interception, and privacy protections of electronic communications

Employee Polygraph Protection Act (EPPA) — prohibition for compulsory lie detector test within the work environment

Employee Retirement Income Security Act of 1974 (ERISA) — welfare benefit plan providing medical, unemployment, vacation, sickness, and other nonretirement benefits

Employer identification number (EIN) — federal tax identification number used to identify a business entity

Equal Employment Opportunity Commission (EEOC) — federal agency charged with responsibility for receiving and investigating charges of discrimination arising under Title VII, the ADA, and the ADEA

Equal Pay Act of 1963 (Equal Pay Act) — prohibition of differences in pay between men and women for the performance of "substantially equal jobs"

Ex officio — by virtue of office; position on a board held by an individual because of his or her position in that or another organization

Excess benefit transaction — financial transaction where benefits provided exceed the fair market value of benefits received

Fair Credit Reporting Act — requirement for an employer to get a written permission from an employee or an applicant before obtaining a credit report

Fair Labor Standards Act (FLSA) — federal law governing employee wages, permitted work hours, and basic employee record keeping

Family & Medical Leave Act of 1993 (FMLA) — federal law protecting employment and providing 12 weeks of unpaid leave for qualified employees after childbirth; adoption; medical recovery; or care of a seriously ill child, spouse, or parent in organizations with over 50 employees

Fiduciary — trustee or guardian with rights and powers normally belonging to another person; obligation to hold those rights for the benefit of the beneficiary

Form 990 — annual information return that most nonprofits must file with the IRS

Form 990-PF — annual information return that private foundations must file with the IRS

Form 990-T — tax return form for tax-exempt nonprofits that generate unrelated business income

Form 1023 — application form for organizations wishing to become recognized by the IRS as a 501(c)(3) tax-exempt organization

Form 1024 — application form for organizations wishing to become recognized by the IRS as a tax-exempt organization other than those described in Section 501(c)(3)

Form 5500 — annual information return filed by the employer on behalf of employee benefit plans

Gift-in-kind — charitable gift of property or service

Governance — legal authority of a board to establish policies that will affect the life and work of the organization while holding the board accountable for the outcome of such decisions

Grass-roots lobbying — effort to influence legislation via appeals to the general public to contact legislators

Health Insurance Portability and Accountability Act (HIPAA) — privacy protection for an individual's health care information

Incorporator — individual who organizes a corporation

Indemnification — "holding harmless"; promise of a nonprofit to pay legal costs for claims that result from service on behalf of the organization

Independent contractor — individual who is contracted to perform a specific project or service according to his own methods for a specified amount; not an employee

Intermediate sanctions — penalty excise taxes imposed by the IRS on insiders in a tax-exempt organization for violations pertaining to excessive financial transactions

Joint venture — collaboration between two or more individuals or organizations with the intent to carry out a business venture for their joint profit

Liability — legal responsibility for an act or failure to act

Limited liability company (LLC) — form of business structure offering the beneficial tax status of a partnership while providing its members limited liability

Limited partnership — partnership where some partners' liability is limited to the amount of initial investment

Litigation — dispute handled through a lawsuit in a court

Lobbying — effort to influence legislation

Merger — consolidation of two or more organizations where the new merged entity becomes the owner and responsible for all the assets and liabilities

Nonprofit — organization defined by state law whose income is distributed for permitted purposes and not to its members; not a for-profit or a government entity

Occupational Safety & Health Act (OSHA) — act requiring provision of safe working conditions for employees

Officer — usually a board member with additional duties and specific authority to represent the organization

Older Worker Benefit Protection Act (OWBPA) — amendment to the ADEA providing guidelines for procedures and disclosures when an older worker is let go because of organizational downsizing

Operational test — IRS requirement for a public charity to operate primarily for charitable purposes and to benefit the public at large, not individuals associated with it

Organizational test — requirement for a charity's articles of organization to define the organizational purposes and provisions for dissolution according to limitations set by the IRS

Patent — protection for inventors granting the exclusive right to make, use, or sell to exclude outsiders from making, using, or selling the patented invention for a term of years

Pension benefit plan — benefit plan providing retirement income to employees

Political Action Committee (PAC) — separate segregated fund whose function is to influence federal, state, or local public office elections

Private foundation — tax-exempt 501(c)(3) organization, other than a public charity, with funds usually from a single source and established to maintain or aid charitable activities serving the common good, primarily through grantmaking

Private inurement — excessive benefit (greater than what he or she provides in return) to an insider, an individual who has substantial influence over the organization

Profit sharing plan — similar to a defined contribution retirement plan; funded by an employer with discretionary contributions to employees' accounts

Public charity — 501(c)(3) tax-exempt organization that receives broad support from the general public

Public support test — calculation allowing the IRS to differentiate between a public charity and a private foundation

Qualified pension plan — benefit plan that complies with IRS requirements and does not favor highly compensated employees

Quid pro quo — fair exchange; contribution for which the organization returns some benefit to the giver

Quorum — minimum number of members entitled to vote who must be present at a meeting before any business can be transacted legally

Robert's Rules of Order — parliamentary procedure used to conduct meetings

Robinson-Patman Act — protection for small retailers by prohibiting price discrimination by manufacturers

Royalty — payment to copyright owners for the sale or use of their work

Sarbanes-Oxley Act — landmark corporate reform legislation of 2002

Search warrant — court order obtained by prosecutors to give law enforcement agents the right to enter the premises mentioned in the warrant

Section 1981 of the Reconstruction Era Civil Rights Act (Section 1981) — prohibition of racial and national origin discrimination in the making and enforcement of contracts

Self-dealing — situation where an organizational insider is engaged in a financial transaction as the provider and receiver of the benefit

Self-perpetuating board — governing board where the board members are able to elect subsequent members

Sherman Act — law prohibiting adverse effect on competition and formation of monopolies

Social welfare organization — nonprofit organization furthering the common good and general welfare of the people in a community

SS-4 — form every organization needs to file with the IRS to receive its own employer identification number (EIN), whether there are employees or not

Subpoena — order of court to obligate an individual to testify or produce documents by a certain date

Tax-deductible donation — donation that a donor can deduct from his or her taxable income

Tax exemption — exemption of a nonprofit organization from paying a variety of federal, state, and/or local taxes

Title VII — federal Civil Rights Act provisions prohibiting discrimination based on race, color, religion, sex, or national origin in hiring, discharge, compensation, and any terms, conditions, or privileges of employment

Tort — a civil wrong or injury, other than breach of contract, which a court can remedy through an award of damages

Trade association — individuals and companies in a specific business or industry organized to promote common interests

Trademark — word, symbol, design, or a combination thereof, that identifies and distinguishes a person's or an organization's goods or services from those of another

Uniformed Services Employment and Reemployment Rights Act (USERRA) — prohibition of discrimination against employees committed to serving in the military forces; protection of seniority and certain benefits

Unincorporated association — agreement between individuals to come together to fulfill a specific purpose without any organizational legal identity or liability protection for involved individuals

Unrelated business income — income from business activities that are not substantially mission related

Unrelated business income tax (UBIT) — tax obligation for income over $1,000 raised from unrelated business activities

Welfare benefit plan — plan providing employee benefits such as health care, vacation, and life insurance

Appendix III: Sample Whistleblower Policy

General

[Organization name] ("Organization") Code of Ethics and Conduct ("Code") requires directors, officers, and employees to observe high standards of business and personal ethics in the conduct of their duties and responsibilities. As employees and representatives of the Organization, we must practice honesty and integrity in fulfilling our responsibilities and comply with all applicable laws and regulations.

Reporting Responsibility

It is the responsibility of all directors, officers, and employees to comply with the Code and to report violations or suspected violations in accordance with this Whistleblower Policy.

No Retaliation

No director, officer, or employee who in good faith reports a violation of the Code shall suffer harassment, retaliation, or adverse employment consequence. An employee who retaliates against someone who has reported a violation in good faith is subject to discipline up to and including termination of employment. This Whistleblower Policy is intended to encourage and enable employees and others to raise serious concerns within the Organization prior to seeking resolution outside the Organization.

Reporting Violations

The Code addresses the Organization's open door policy and suggests that employees share their questions, concerns, suggestions or complaints with someone who can address them properly. In most cases, an employee's supervisor is in the best position to address an area of concern. However, if you are not comfortable speaking with your supervisor or you are not satisfied with your supervisor's response, you are encouraged to speak with someone in the Human Resources Department or anyone in management whom you are comfortable in approaching. Supervisors and managers are required to report suspected violations of the Code of Conduct to the Organization's Compliance Officer, who has specific and exclusive responsibility to investigate all reported violations. For suspected fraud, or when you are not satisfied or uncomfortable with following the Organization's open door policy, individuals should contact the Organization's Compliance Officer directly.

Compliance Officer

The Organization's Compliance Officer is responsible for investigating and resolving all reported complaints and allegations concerning violations of the Code and, at his discretion, shall advise the Executive Director and/or the audit committee. The Compliance Officer has direct access to the audit committee of the board of directors and is required to report to the audit committee at least annually on compliance activity. The Organization's Compliance Officer is the chair of the audit committee.

Accounting and Auditing Matters

The audit committee of the board of directors shall address all reported concerns or complaints regarding corporate accounting practices, internal controls, or auditing. The Compliance Officer shall immediately notify the audit committee of any such complaint and work with the committee until the matter is resolved.

Acting in Good Faith

Anyone filing a complaint concerning a violation or suspected violation of the Code must be acting in good faith and have reasonable grounds for believing the information disclosed indicates a violation of the Code. Any allegations that prove not to be substantiated and which prove to have been made maliciously or knowingly to be false will be viewed as a serious disciplinary offense.

Confidentiality

Violations or suspected violations may be submitted on a confidential basis by the complainant or may be submitted anonymously. Reports of violations or suspected violations will be kept confidential to the extent possible, consistent with the need to conduct an adequate investigation.

Handling of Reported Violations

The Compliance Officer will notify the sender and acknowledge receipt of the reported violation or suspected violation within five business days. All reports will be promptly investigated and appropriate corrective action will be taken if warranted by the investigation.

_____

Audit Committee Compliance Officer

_____

[Organization name] Management Staff

SUGGESTED RESOURCES

Fletcher, Kathleen. *The Policy Sampler: A Resource for Nonprofit Boards*. Washington, DC: BoardSource, 2000. In addition to steering an organization's activities, nonprofit boards are also responsible for setting policies that govern their own actions. This resource provides nonprofit leaders with more than 70 sample board policies and job descriptions collected from a wide variety of nonprofits. The user's guide provides a basic overview for each of the policies. An accompanying CD-ROM contains the full selection of sample policies and job descriptions that can be easily customized to suit your organization.

Hopkins, Bruce R. *The First Legal Answer Book for Fund-Raisers*. New York: John Wiley & Sons, 2000. As the competition for gifts continues to grow, executives and fundraisers for charitable organizations must learn how to work with tax and business law to optimize their return. In a question-and-answer format, Bruce Hopkins clearly explains to fundraisers significant aspects of the law, and thoroughly details the steps needed to solve fundraisers' most pressing legal issues.

Hopkins, Bruce R. *Legal Responsibilities of Nonprofit Boards*. Washington, DC: BoardSource, 2003. All board members should understand their legal responsibilities, including when and how they can be held personally liable and what type of oversight they should provide. Discover the essential information that board members should know to protect themselves and their organization. Written in non-technical language, this book provides legal concepts and definitions, as well as a detailed discussion on ethics.

Hopkins, Bruce R. *Starting and Managing a Nonprofit Organization: A Legal Guide, 4th Edition*. New York: John Wiley & Sons, 2004. This essential resource covers virtually every legal aspect of starting and operating a nonprofit organization, public or private, and has been revised and expanded to include updated information on recent changes involving nonprofit governance. Bruce Hopkins gives you practical guidance on the rules and regulations governing nonprofits and up-to-date information on reporting revenue, private benefits, personal liability, charitable giving rules, employee compensation, lobbying, and for-profit subsidiaries. The book also includes useful checklists and a glossary of legal terms.

Ingram, Richard T. *Ten Basic Responsibilities of Nonprofit Boards*. Washington, DC: BoardSource, 2003. More than 150,000 board members have already discovered this #1 BoardSource bestseller. This newly revised edition explores the 10 core areas of board responsibility. Share with board members the basic responsibilities, including determining mission and purpose, ensuring effective planning, and participating in fundraising. You'll find that this is an ideal reference for drafting job descriptions, assessing board performance, and orienting board members on their responsibilities.

Jacobs, Jerald. *Association Law Handbook, Third Edition*. Washington, DC: American Society of Association Executives, 1996. Written for association executives as well as attorneys, this compact, quick-reference handbook makes association law accessible and easy to understand. Each chapter includes a resource guide directing you to additional books, articles, cases, laws, and regulations, plus you'll find sample association documents including articles of incorporation, bylaws, guidelines for antitrust, and an association chief executive employment contract. This book serves as an outstanding hands-on manual or library reference.

Kurtz, Daniel L. *Managing Conflicts of Interest: Practical Guidelines for Nonprofit Boards*. Washington, DC: BoardSource, 2001. Attorney Daniel Kurtz helps board members understand exactly what constitutes a conflict of interest. He explains the legal context of the conflict, offers examples, and suggests guidelines on how to manage them. The book includes a CD-ROM that contains sample conflict-of-interest policies and statements.

Tesdahl, D. Benson. *The Nonprofit Board's Guide to Bylaws: Creating a Framework for Effective Governance*. Washington, DC: BoardSource, 2003. It is important that your board periodically review and adjust its bylaws in response to organizational change and growth. This newly revised book will help your board determine how your organization is best structured, the rights of the participants within the structure, and important organizational procedures. Included in the text are findings from a BoardSource conducted survey, providing recent empirical data about how nonprofits handle certain issues. Don't miss the sample bylaws provisions and the conflicts-of-interest policies on the accompanying CD-ROM!

About the Firm

Founded in 1903, Ober|Kaler has more than 120 attorneys, and offices in Maryland, Washington D.C., and Virginia. Clients across the country and around the world look to Ober|Kaler for outstanding skills and knowledge of regulatory and transactional issues, litigation, and the depth of its resources in other key areas of the law. Ober|Kaler represents a wide variety of tax-exempt organizations and associations, including foundations, universities, schools, public charities, religious organizations, trade and professional associations, national health advocacy and provider organizations, scientific associations and consortia, and cultural and arts organizations. It recognizes the dedication of clients to their missions, their increasing importance in society, and the complexity of the regulatory and business challenges they face. The attorneys at Ober|Kaler assist clients through the provision of a complete complement of efficient and effective legal services in the areas of taxation, corporate matters, governance and management, intellectual property, employment matters, employee benefits, antitrust, immigration matters, government relations, white collar defense, and litigation. The firm is committed to integrity and value.

For more information, contact Ober|Kaler at mechambers@ober.com.

ABOUT THOMAS K. HYATT (GENERAL EDITOR)

Tom Hyatt is a shareholder in the law firm of Ober|Kaler, resident in the Washington, D.C. office. His practice has focused on corporate and tax-exempt organization issues for health care providers. A substantial portion of Tom's practice involves counseling nonprofit organizations on governance and transactional matters. He frequently works with nonprofit governing boards and board committees to address such issues as regulatory compliance, fiduciary duty, conflicts of interest, bylaws development and revision, senior management compensation and benefits, chief executive transition, fundraising, lobbying and political campaign activity, board development, membership matters, corporate restructuring, mergers, and joint ventures. He is admitted to practice in the District of Columbia and Pennsylvania.

Mr. Hyatt is a 1979 *cum laude* graduate of Boston College, and received his law degree in 1982 from the University of Pittsburgh, where he served as editor-in-chief of the *Journal of Law and Commerce*. He is a member of the American Health Lawyers Association (AHLA) and is also a member of the American Bar Association and the District of Columbia Bar. He is admitted to the bar in the District of Columbia and in Pennsylvania. In 2004, Mr. Hyatt received AHLA's David J. Greenburg Service Award. He is listed in the 2005–2006 edition of *Best Lawyers in America*. He currently serves on the Advisory Board of the *Journal of Health Law* and the *Exempt Organizations Tax Review*.